EASY PIANO

# FIRST 50
# BROADWAY SONGS

## YOU SHOULD PLAY ON THE PIANO

ISBN 978-1-4950-3590-6

7777 W. BLUEMOUND RD. P.O. BOX 13819 MILWAUKEE, WI 53213

Visit Hal Leonard Online at
**www.halleonard.com**

Contact us:
**Hal Leonard**
7777 West Bluemound Road
Milwaukee, WI 53213
Email: info@halleonard.com

In Europe, contact:
**Hal Leonard Europe Limited**
42 Wigmore Street
Marylebone, London, W1U 2RN
Email: info@halleonardeurope.com

In Australia, contact:
**Hal Leonard Australia Pty. Ltd.**
4 Lentara Court
Cheltenham, Victoria, 3192 Australia
Email: info@halleonard.com.au

# CONTENTS

# ALL I ASK OF YOU

## from THE PHANTOM OF THE OPERA

Music by ANDREW LLOYD WEBBER
Lyrics by CHARLES HART
Additional Lyrics by RICHARD STILGOE

**Slowly, in 2**

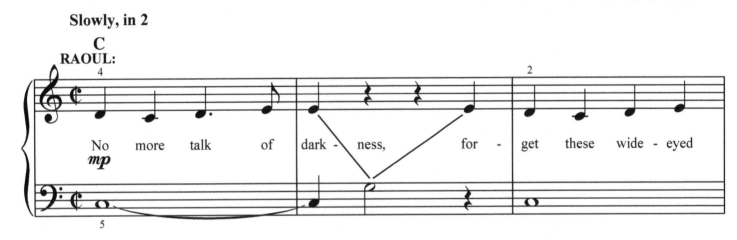

No more talk of dark - ness, for - get these wide - eyed

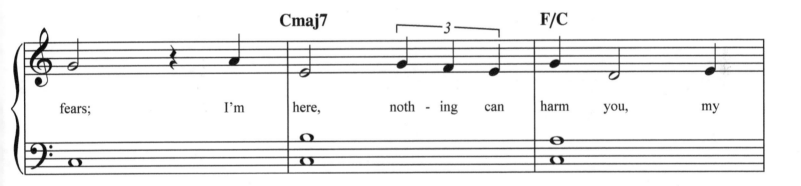

fears; I'm here, noth - ing can harm you, my

words will warm and calm you. Let me be your

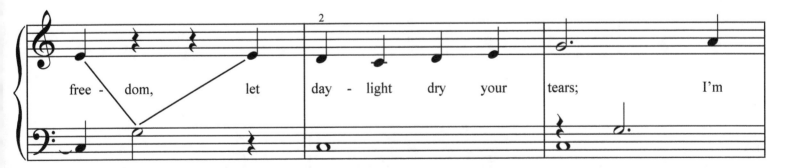

free - dom, let day - light dry your tears; I'm

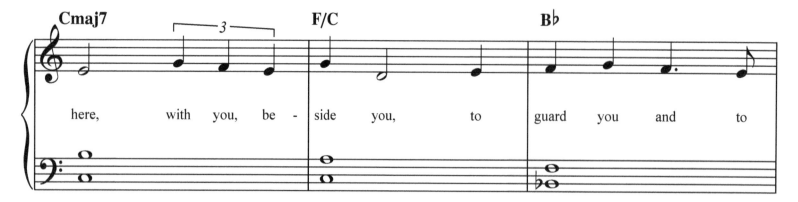

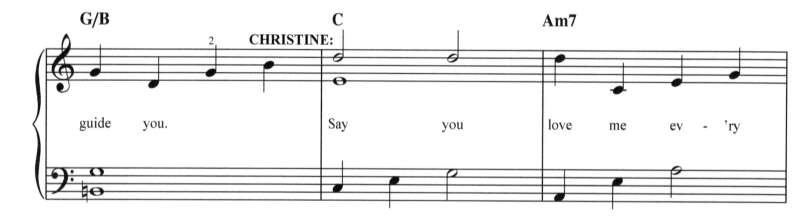

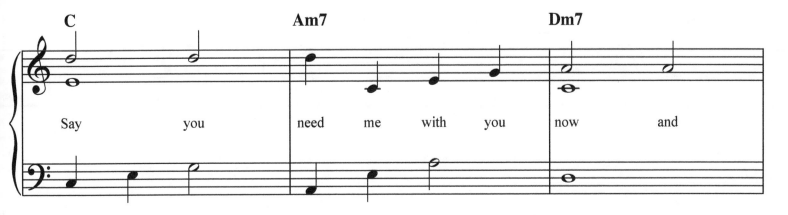

Say you need me with you now and

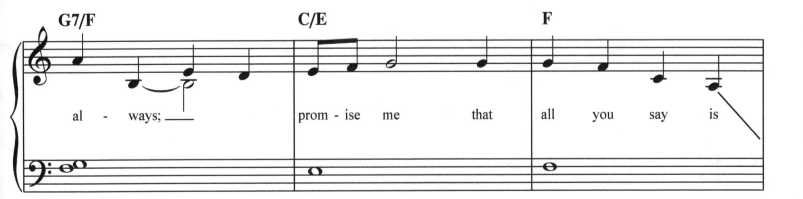

al - ways; ___ prom - ise me that all you say is

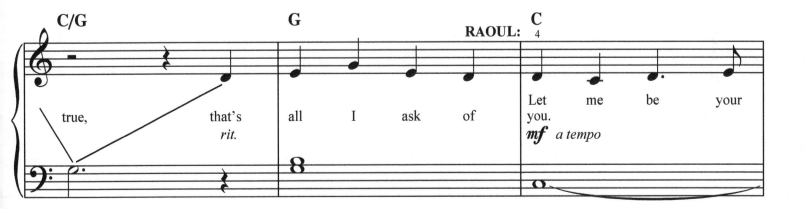

true, that's all I ask of you.

*rit.*

RAOUL: Let me be your

*mf* *a tempo*

shel - ter, let me be your light; you're

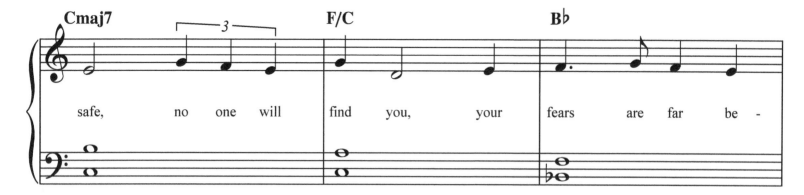

safe, no one will find you, your fears are far be -

**CHRISTINE:**

hind you. All I want is free - dom, a

world with no more night; and you, al - ways be -

**RAOUL:**

side me, to hold me and to hide me. Then

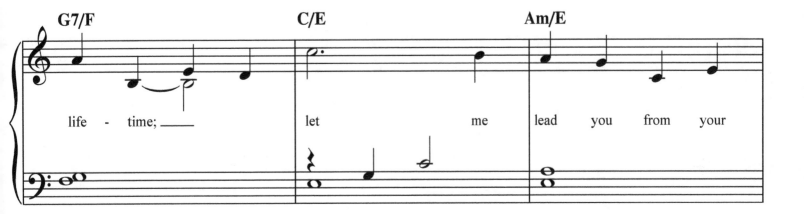

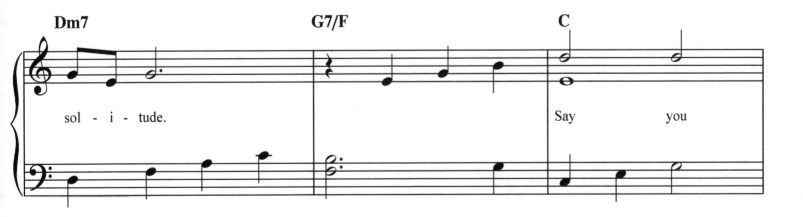

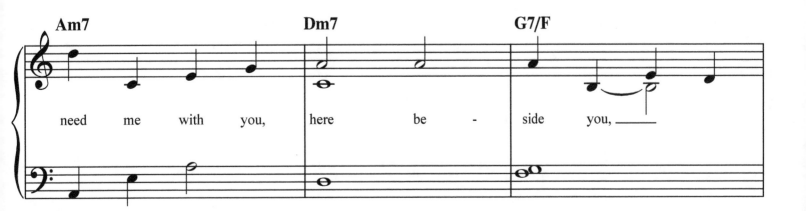

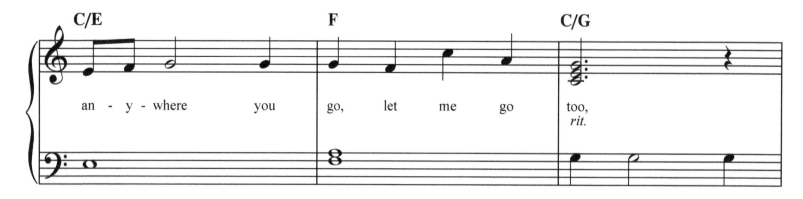

an - y - where you go, let me go too, *rit.*

Chris - tine, that's all I ask of
*molto rit.*

**CHRISTINE:**
Say you'll you.
*f a tempo*
you.

share with me one love, one life - time; ___

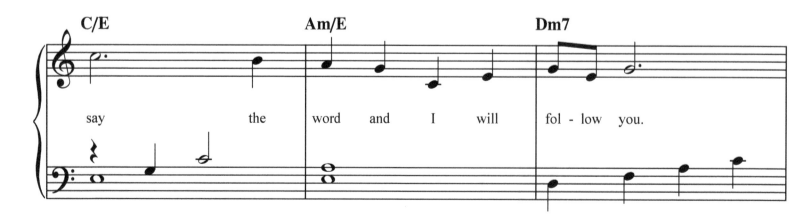

say the word and I will fol - low you.

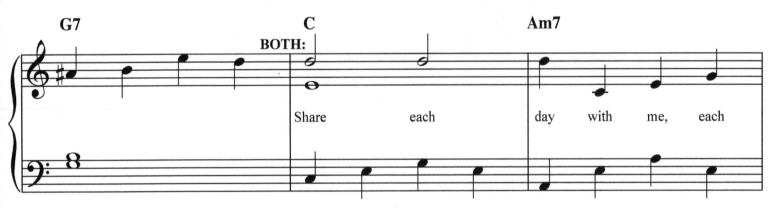

**BOTH:** Share each day with me, each

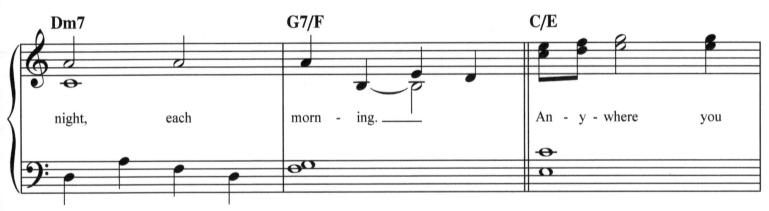

**Slower**

night, each morn - ing. _____ An - y - where you

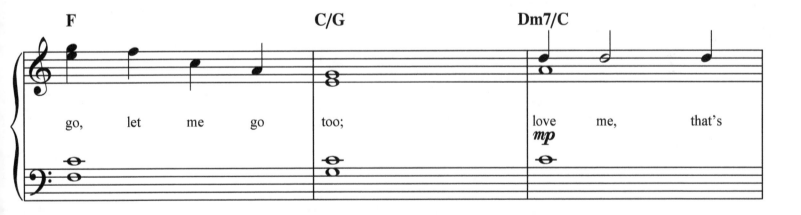

go, let me go too; love me, that's
*mp*

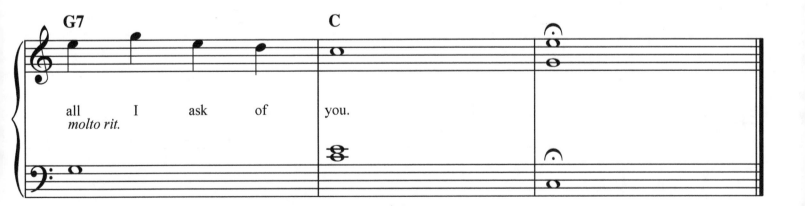

all I ask of you.
*molto rit.*

# ANY DREAM WILL DO

### from JOSEPH AND THE AMAZING TECHNICOLOR® DREAMCOAT

Music by ANDREW LLOYD WEBBER
Lyrics by TIM RICE

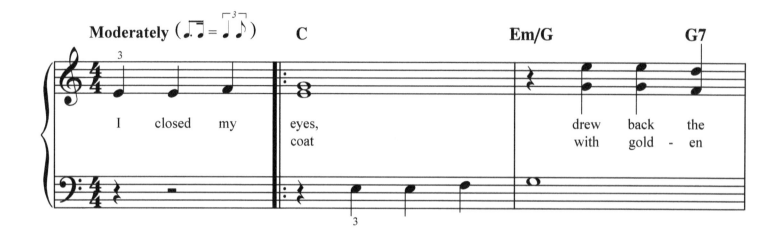

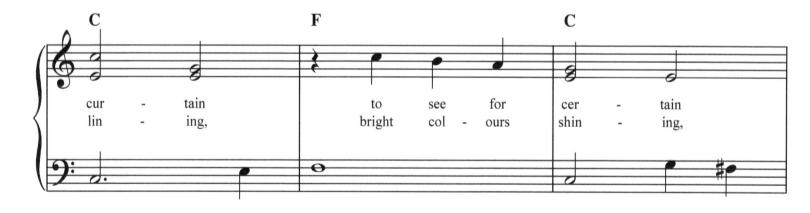

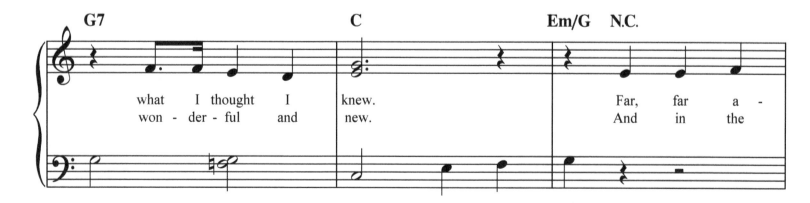

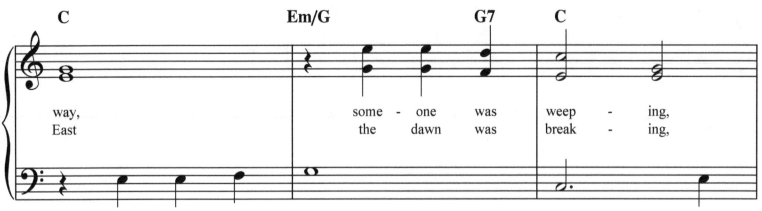

**C**          **Em/G**          **G7**    **C**

way,           some - one    was      weep  -  ing,
East            the    dawn    was     break  -  ing,

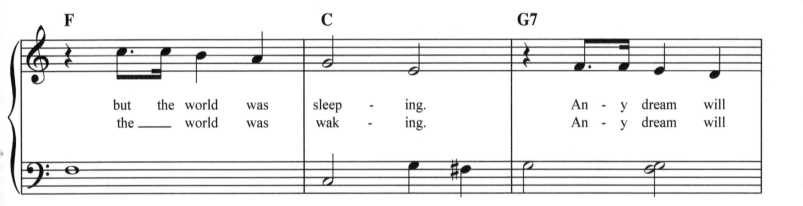

**F**             **C**          **G7**

but    the    world    was      sleep  -  ing.      An - y   dream   will
the     world    was      wak  -  ing.      An - y   dream   will

**1.**
**C**          **Em/G N.C.**        **2.**
                                           **C**         **Bb/C**    **Gm7/C**

do.           I    wore    my       do.                        A

**F**                                              **D7**

crash   of   drums,      a    flash    of    light,      my    gold - en    coat    flew

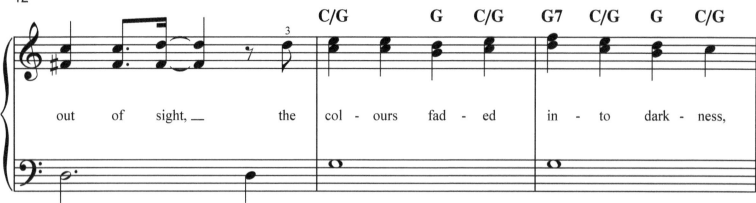

out of sight, ___ the col - ours fad - ed in - to dark - ness,

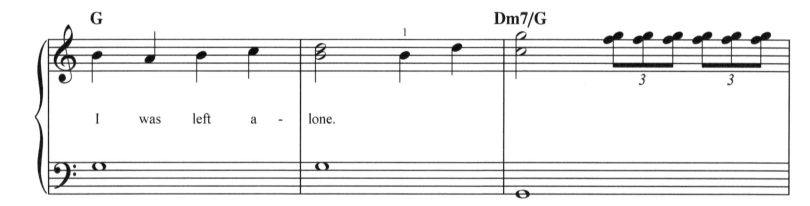

I was left a - lone.

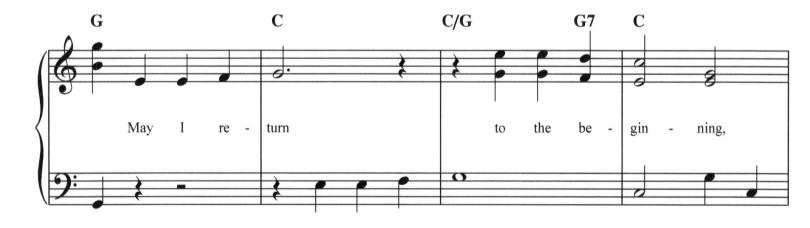

May I re - turn to the be - gin - ning,

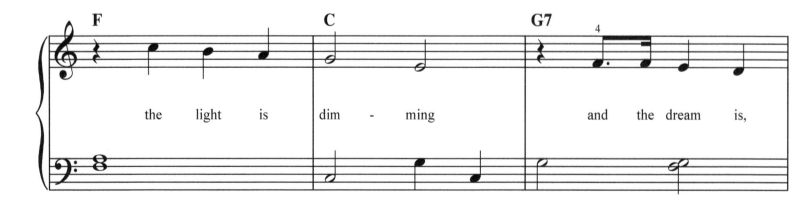

the light is dim - ming and the dream is,

too.

The world and I,

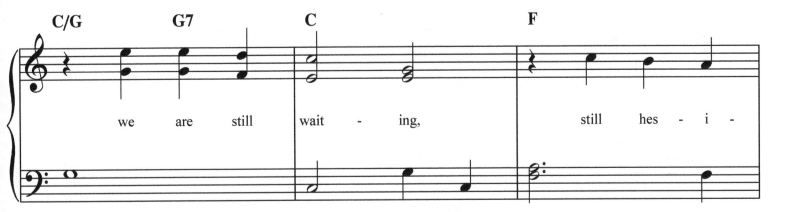

we are still wait - ing,

still hes - i -

tat - ing.

An - y dream will do.

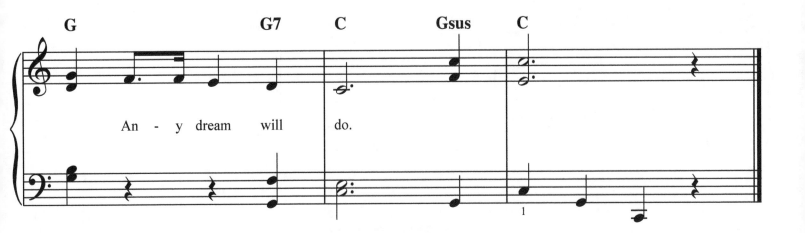

An - y dream will do.

# ANYTHING GOES

## from ANYTHING GOES

Words and Music by
COLE PORTER

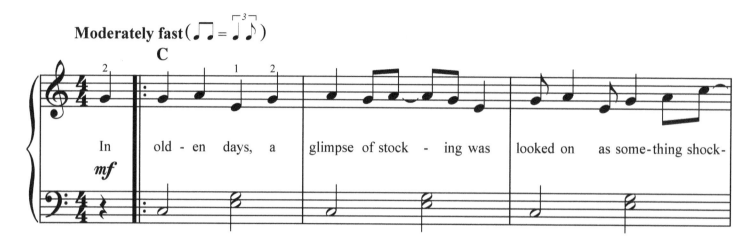

In old-en days, a glimpse of stock-ing was looked on as some-thing shock-

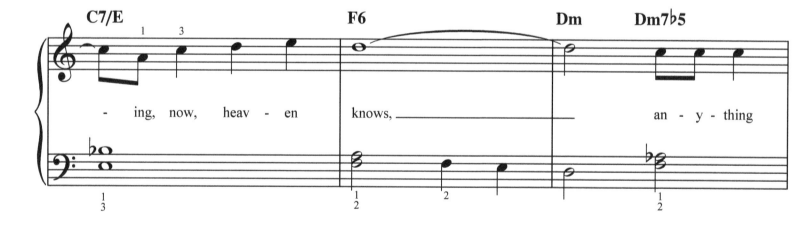

-ing, now, heav-en knows, _____ an-y-thing

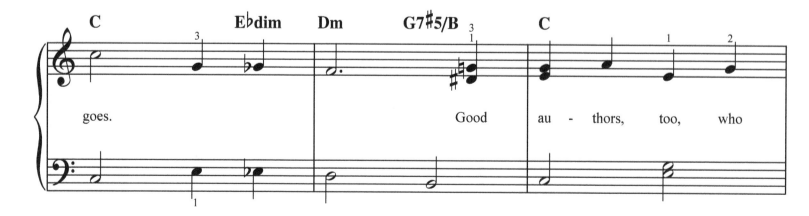

goes. Good au-thors, too, who

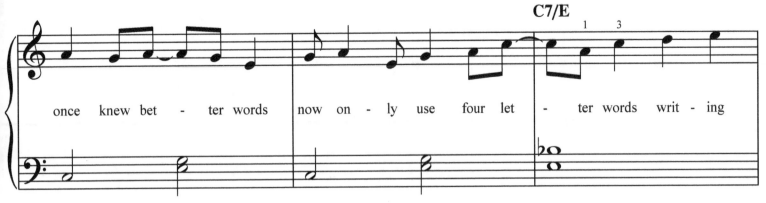

once knew bet - ter words   now on - ly use four let - ter words writ - ing

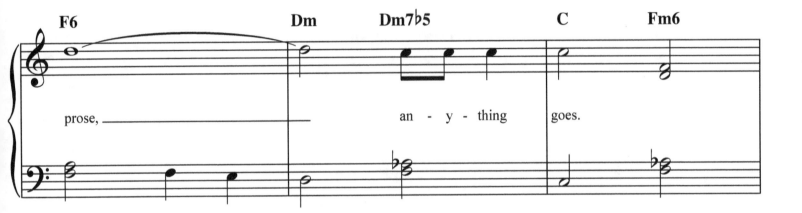

prose, _____   an - y - thing goes.

The world _ has gone   mad to - day, _ and good's   bad to - day, _ and black's

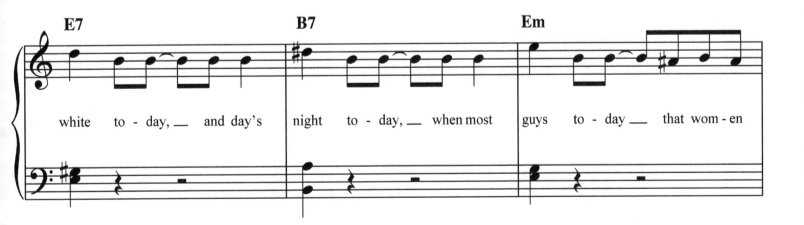

white to - day, _ and day's   night to - day, _ when most   guys to - day _ that wom - en

prize to - day ___ are just sil - ly gi - go - los. ___ So,

though I'm not a great ro - manc - er, I know that {you're / I'm} bound to an -

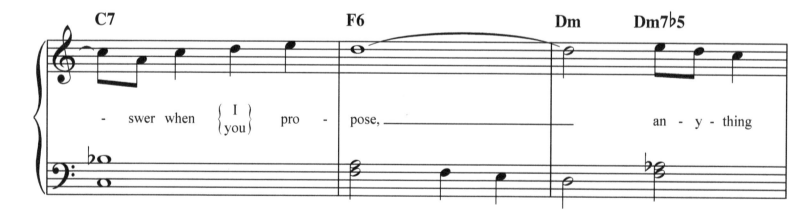

- swer when {I / you} pro - pose, ___ an - y - thing

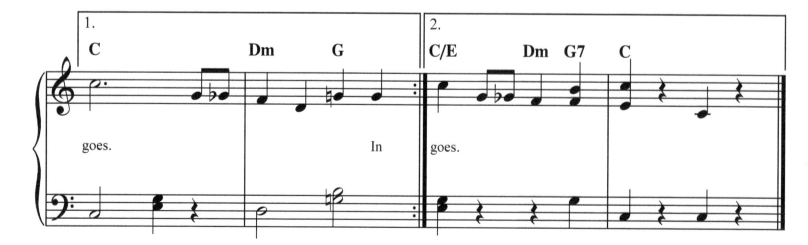

1.
goes.                    In
2.
goes.

# CAN'T HELP LOVIN' DAT MAN

## from SHOW BOAT

Lyrics by OSCAR HAMMERSTEIN II
Music by JEROME KERN

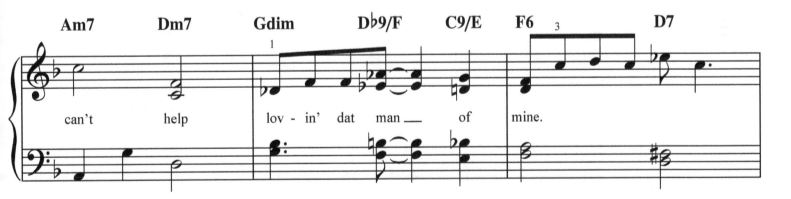

tell me I'm cra - zy, may - be I know, ___ can't help

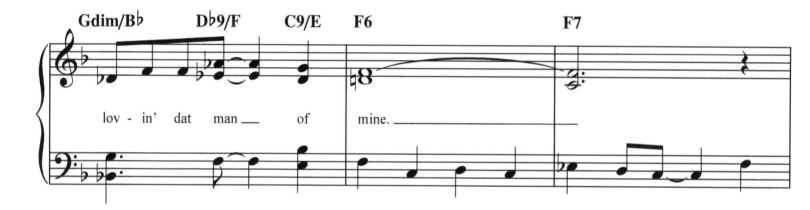

lov - in' dat man ___ of mine. ___

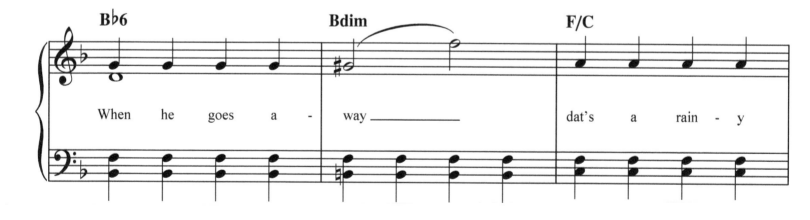

When he goes a - way ___ dat's a rain - y

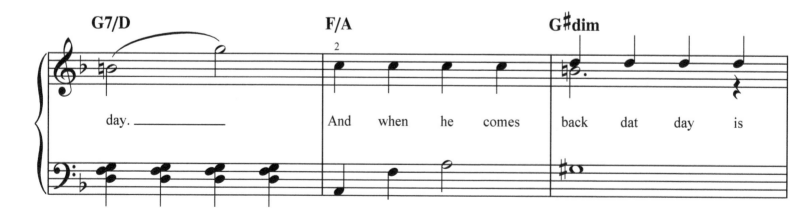

day. ___ And when he comes back dat day is

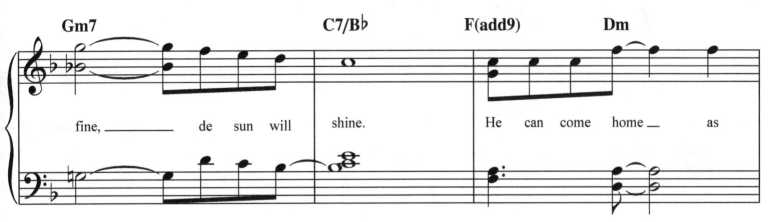

fine, _____ de sun will shine. He can come home _ as

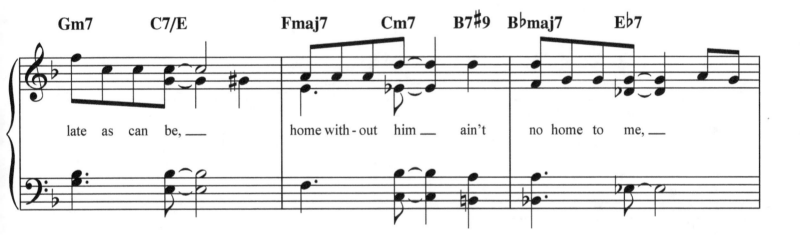

late as can be, ___ home with - out him ___ ain't no home to me, ___

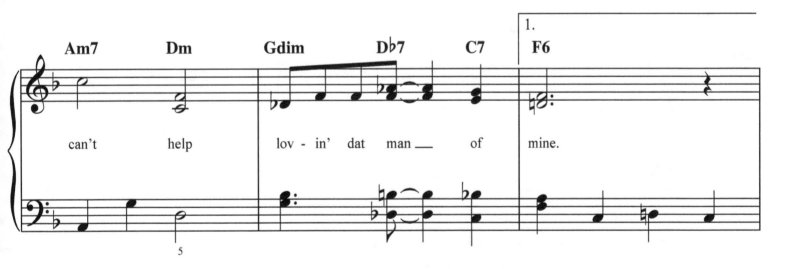

can't help lov - in' dat man _ of mine.

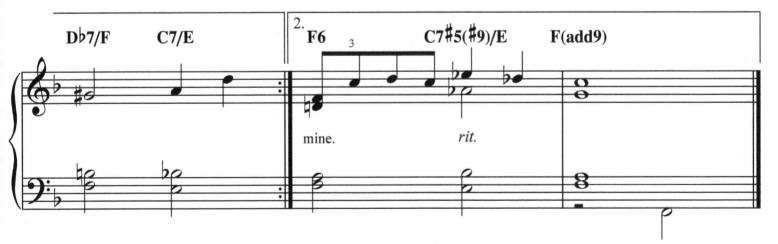

mine. *rit.*

# AS LONG AS HE NEEDS ME

### from the Broadway Musical OLIVER!

Words and Music by
LIONEL BART

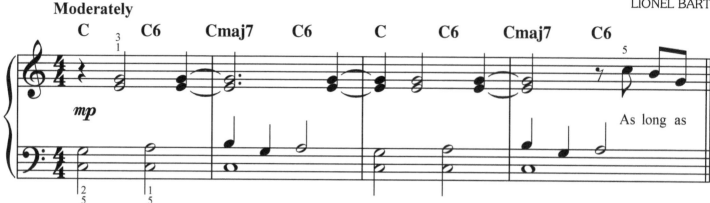

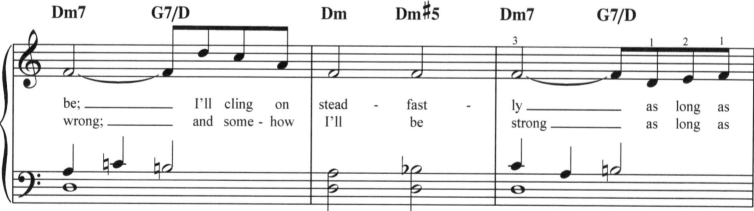

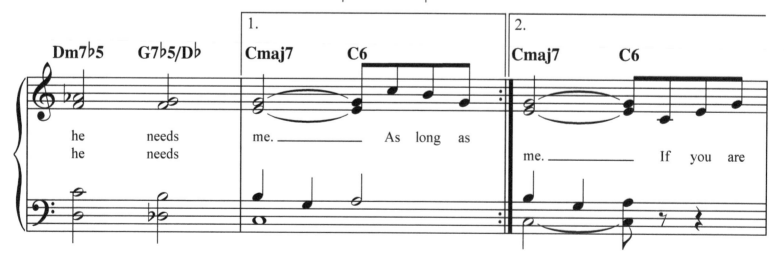

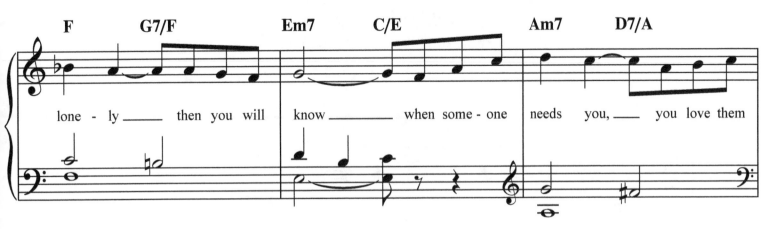

lone - ly _____ then you will know _____ when some - one needs you, _____ you love them

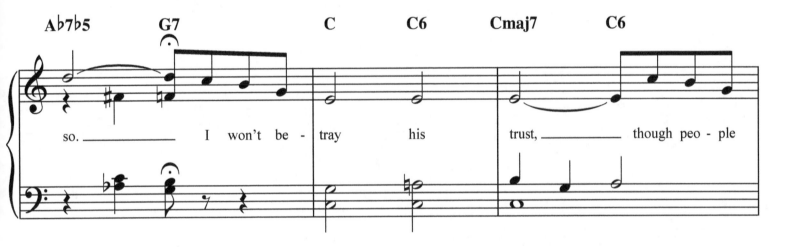

so. _____ I won't be - tray his trust, _____ though peo - ple

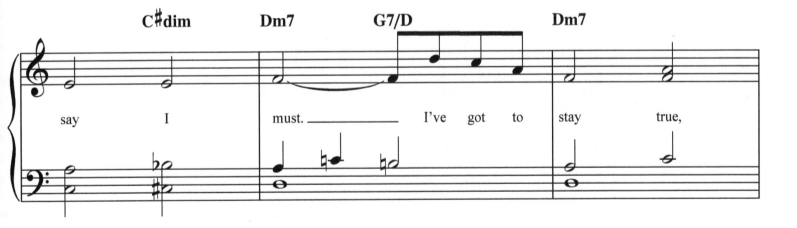

say I must. _____ I've got to stay true,

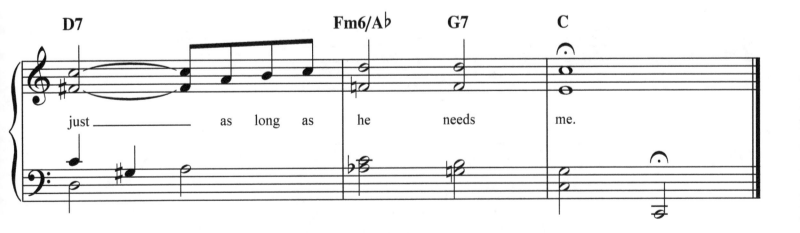

just _____ as long as he needs me.

# CABARET
### from the Musical CABARET

Words by FRED EBB
Music by JOHN KANDER

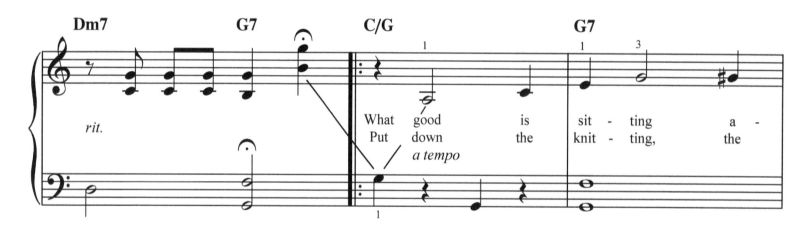

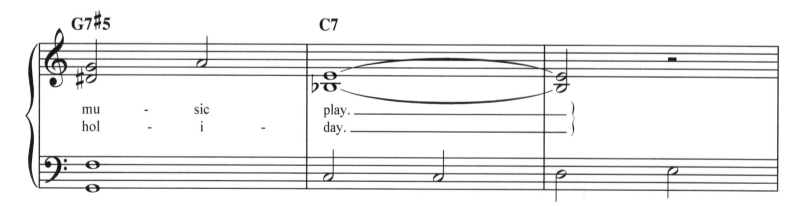

Life is a cab - a - ret, old chum, ___

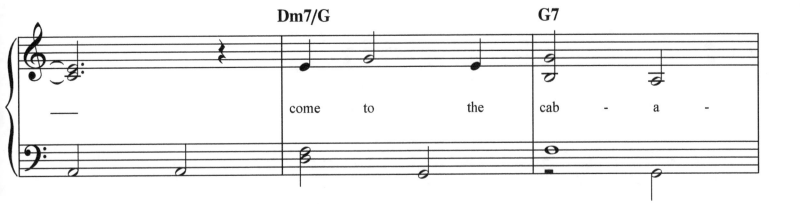

___ come to the cab - a -

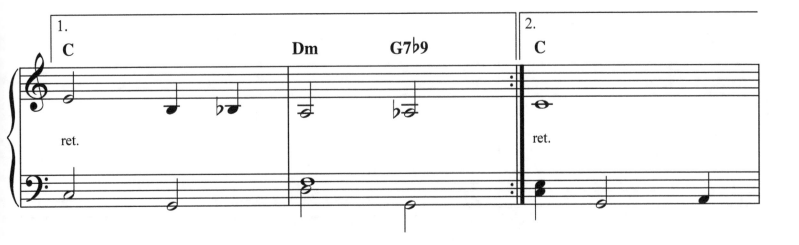

ret. ret.

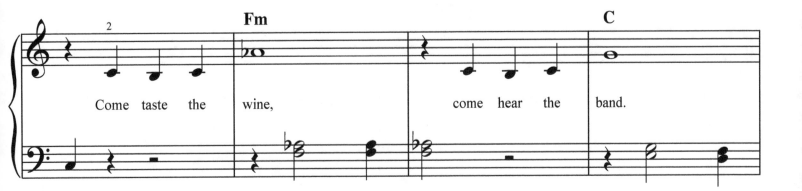

Come taste the wine, come hear the band.

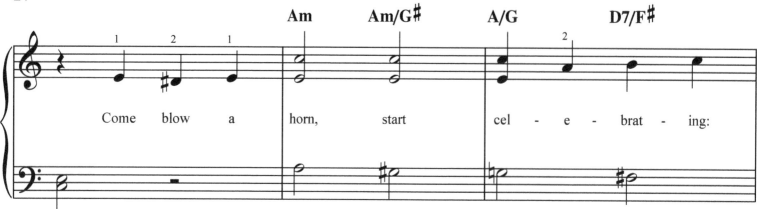

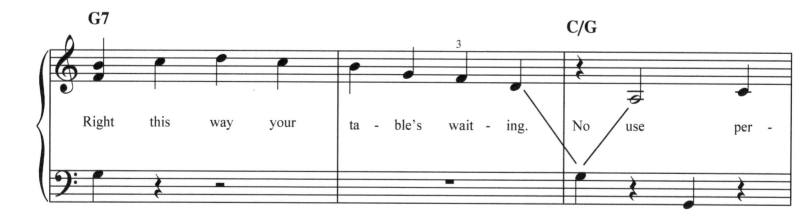

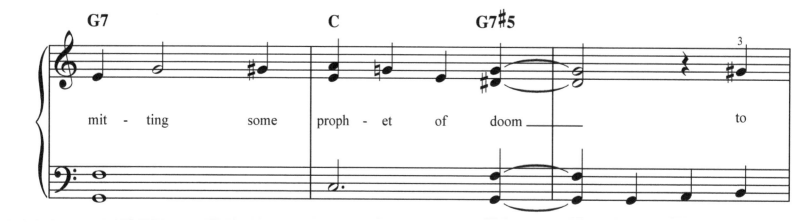

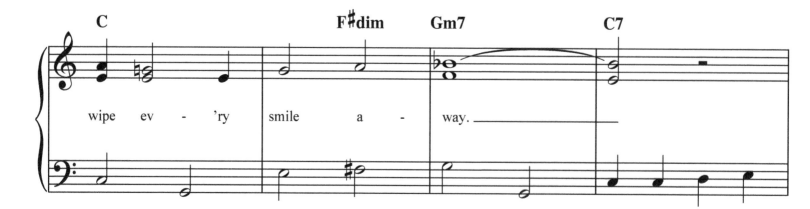

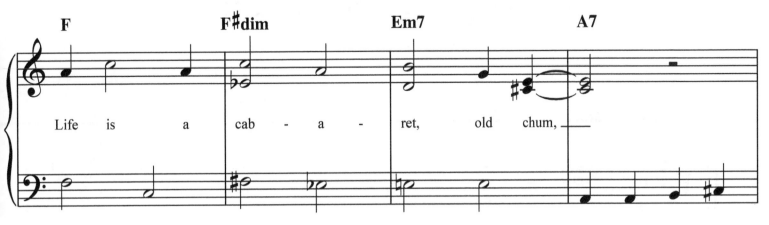

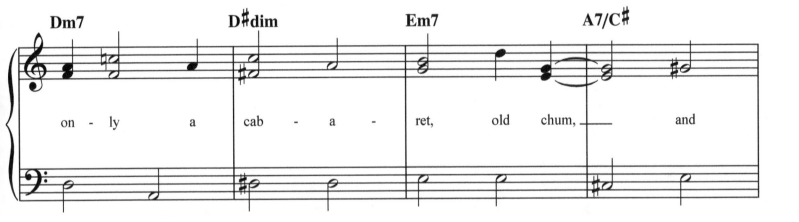

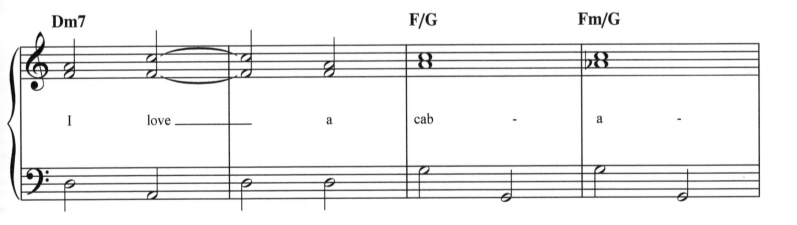

# CONSIDER YOURSELF

**from the Broadway Musical OLIVER!**

Words and Music by
LIONEL BART

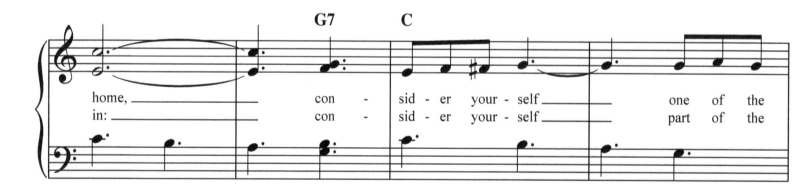

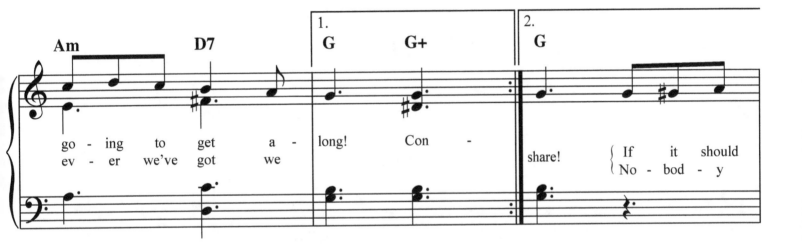

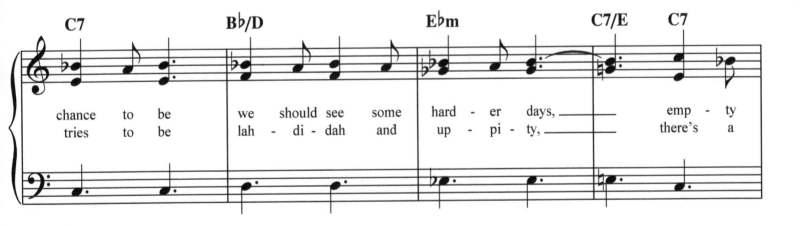

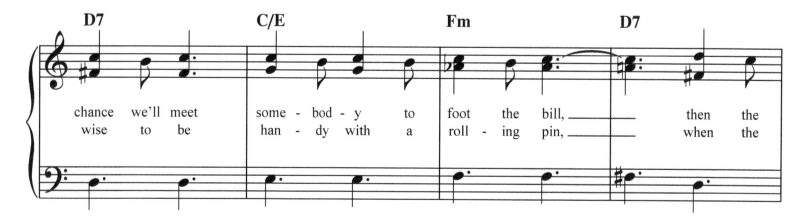

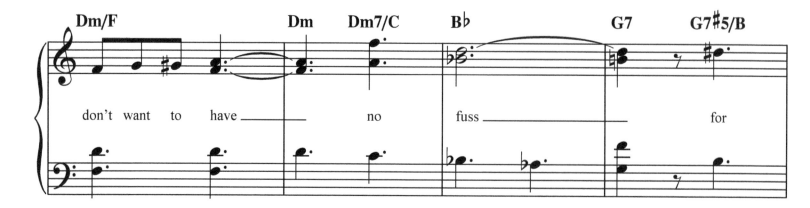

af - ter some con - sid - er - a - tion, we can state: Con -

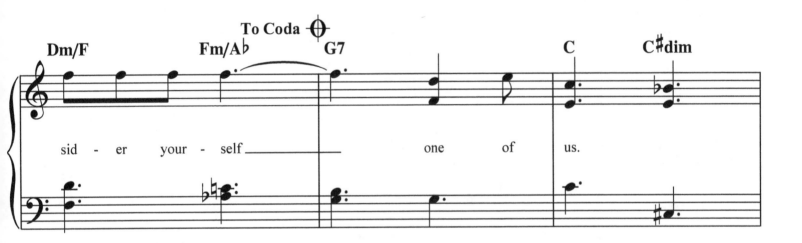

sid - er your - self _____ one of us.

**D.S. al Coda (with repeat)**

Con -

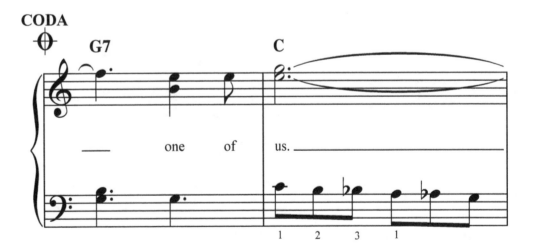

**CODA**

_____ one of us. _____

# DO-RE-MI

### from THE SOUND OF MUSIC

Lyrics by OSCAR HAMMERSTEIN II
Music by RICHARD RODGERS

**With spirit**

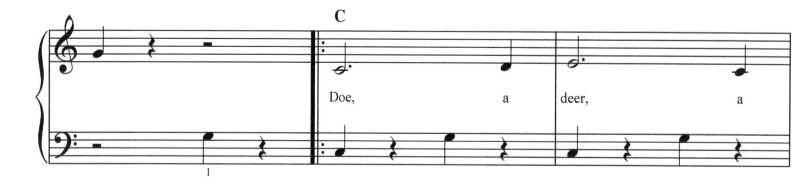

Doe,        a        deer,        a

fe - male        deer,        ray,        a

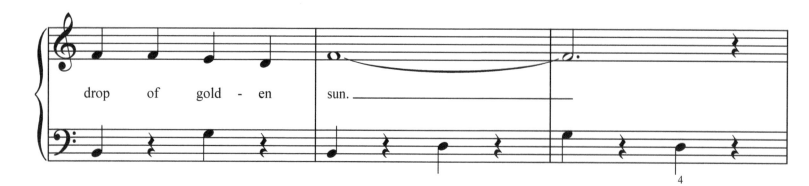

drop    of    gold - en        sun.

Me, a name I call my - self,

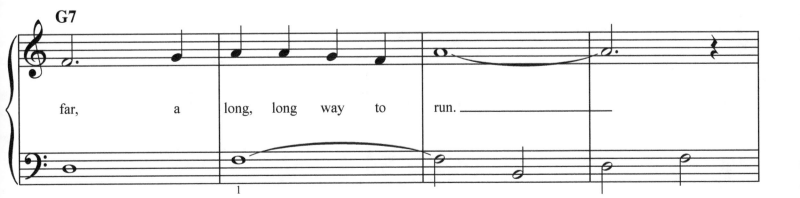

far, a long, long way to run.

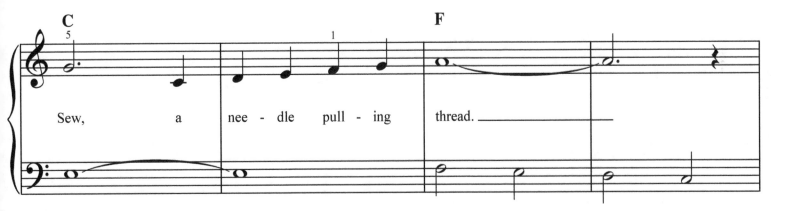

Sew, a nee - dle pull - ing thread.

La, a note to fol - low sew.

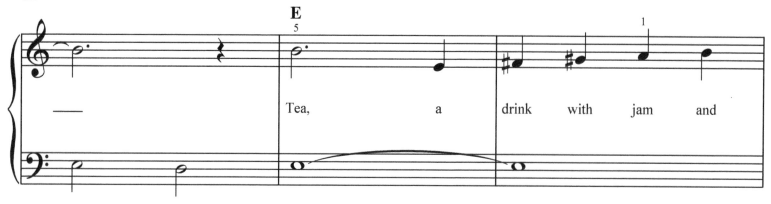

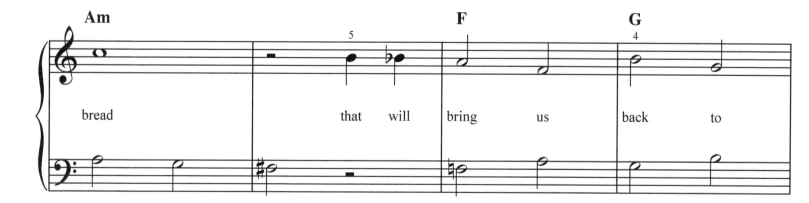

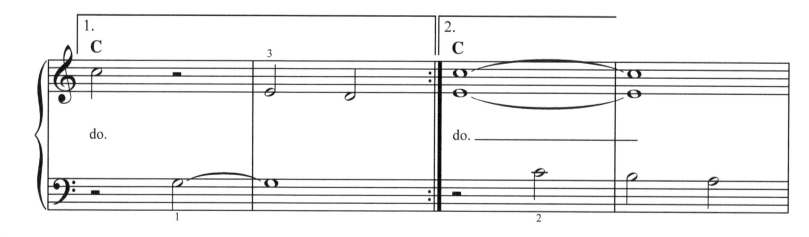

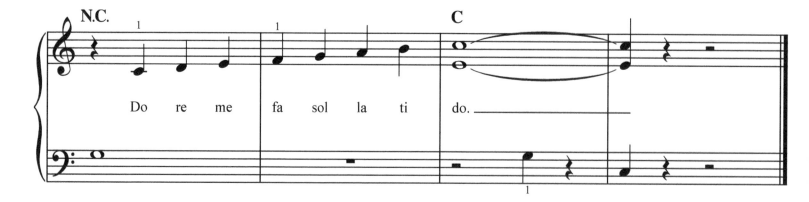

# EDELWEISS
## from THE SOUND OF MUSIC

Lyrics by OSCAR HAMMERSTEIN II
Music by RICHARD RODGERS

**Slowly, with expression**

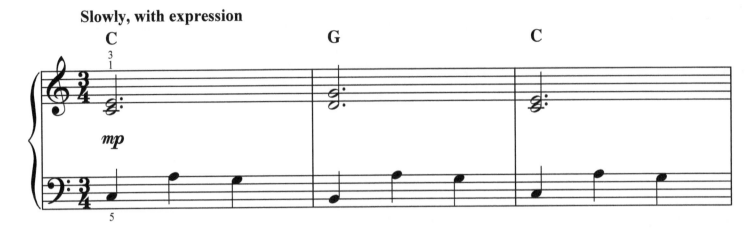

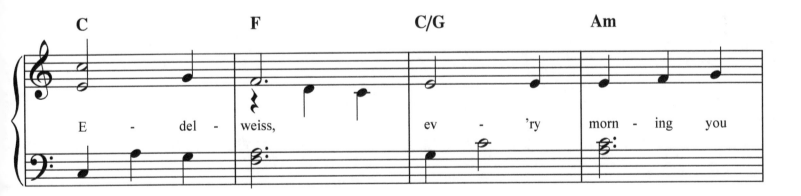

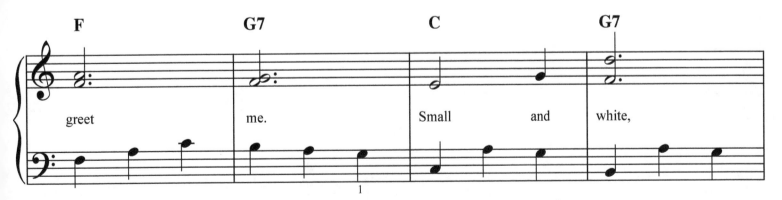

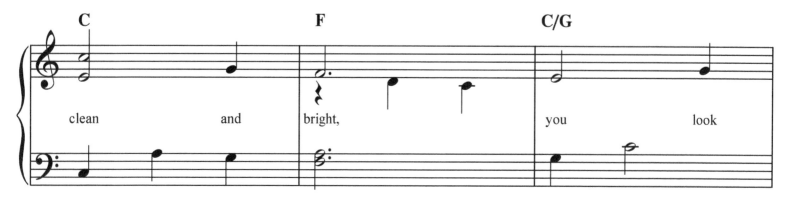

**C**                **F**                **C/G**

clean      and      bright,          you      look

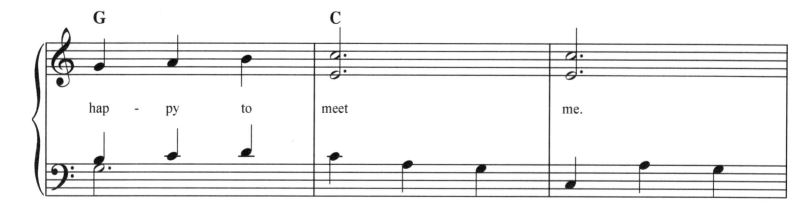

**G**                **C**

hap - py    to      meet        me.

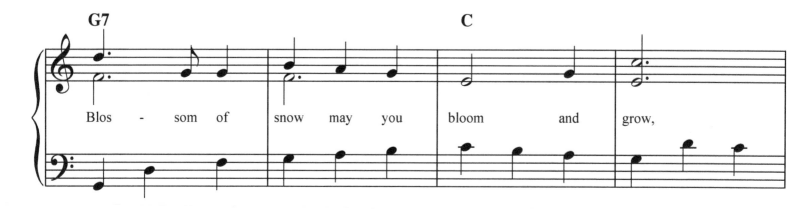

**G7**                        **C**

Blos - som of    snow may you    bloom    and    grow,

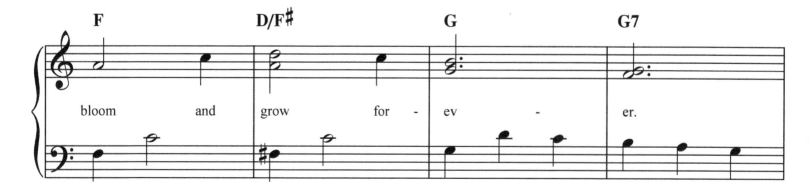

**F**             **D/F♯**             **G**            **G7**

bloom    and    grow    for - ev -    er.

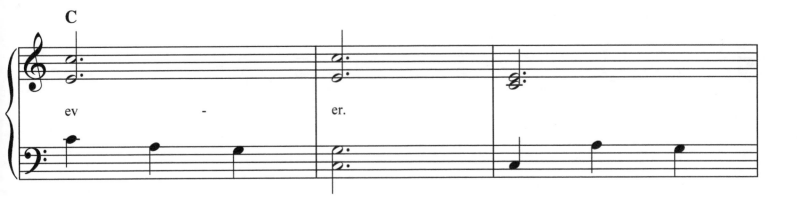

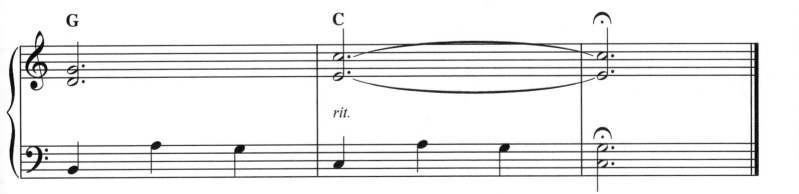

# DO YOU HEAR THE PEOPLE SING?

**from LES MISÉRABLES**

Music by CLAUDE-MICHEL SCHÖNBERG
Lyrics by ALAIN BOUBLIL, JEAN-MARC NATEL
and HERBERT KRETZMER

**Slow March (in 2)**

**ENJOLRAS & STUDENTS:**

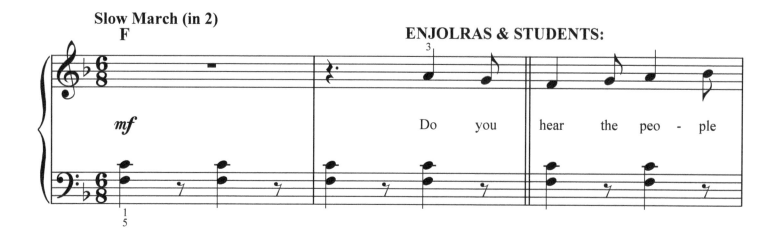

Do you hear the peo - ple

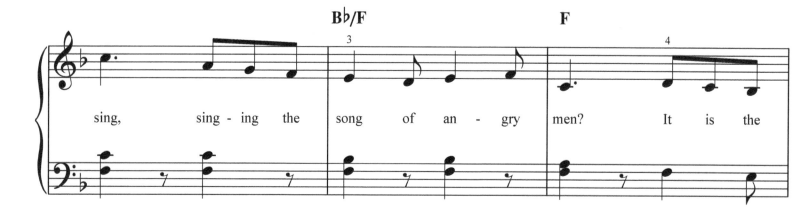

sing, sing - ing the song of an - gry men? It is the

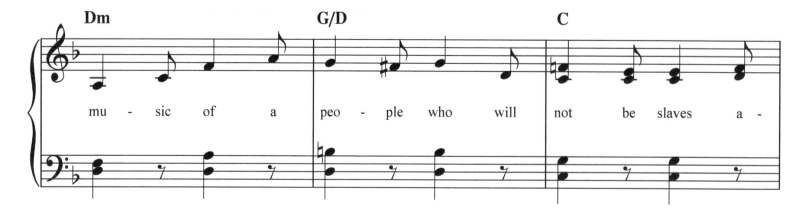

mu - sic of a peo - ple who will not be slaves a -

gain! When the beat - ing of your heart e - choes the

**Bb/F**         **F**         **Dm**

beat - ing of the drums, there is a life a - bout to

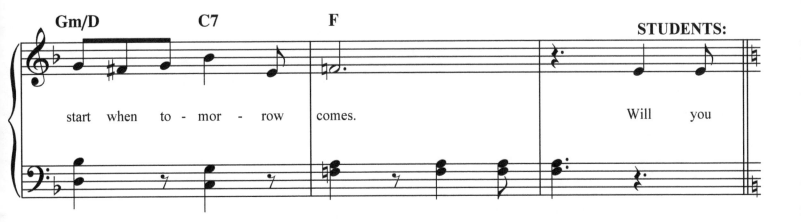

**Gm/D**    **C7**      **F**        **STUDENTS:**

start when to - mor - row comes. Will you

**Am**            **Em**

join in our cru - sade? Who will be strong and stand with
give all you can give so that our ban - ner may ad -

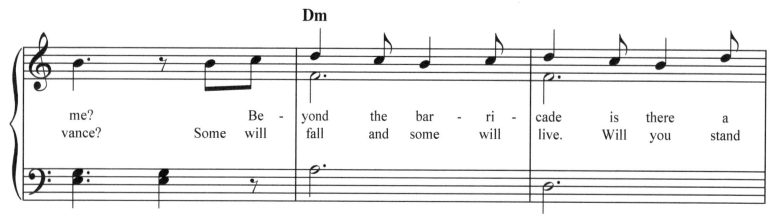

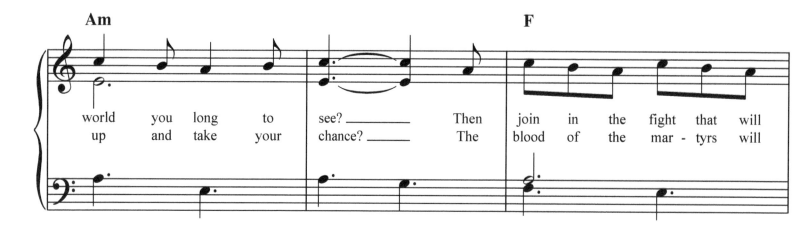

peo - ple who will not be slaves a - gain! When the

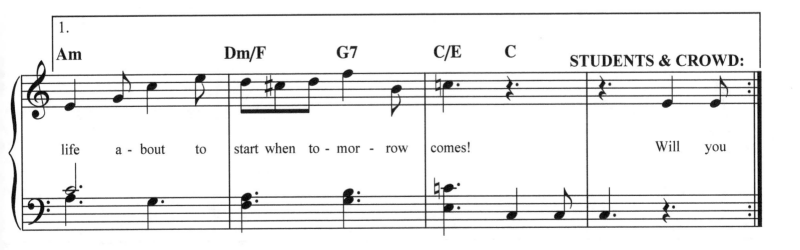

beat - ing of your heart e - choes the beat - ing of the drums, there is a

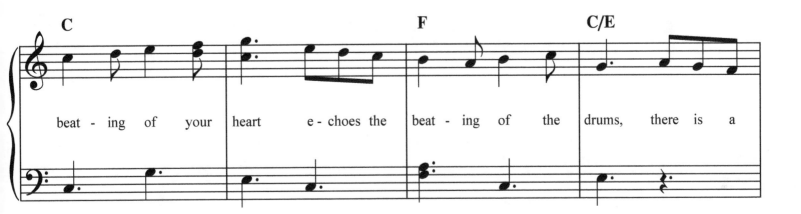

1.

**STUDENTS & CROWD:**

life a - bout to start when to - mor - row comes! Will you

2.

life a - bout to start when to - mor - row comes!

# DON'T CRY FOR ME ARGENTINA
## from EVITA

Words by TIM RICE
Music by ANDREW LLOYD WEBBER

**Moderate Tango**

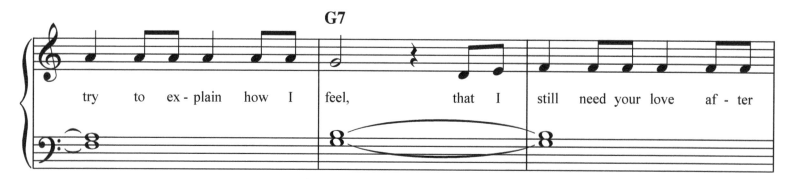

**G/B**           **D7**           **G**

nines     at     six - es   and   sev - ens   with    you.

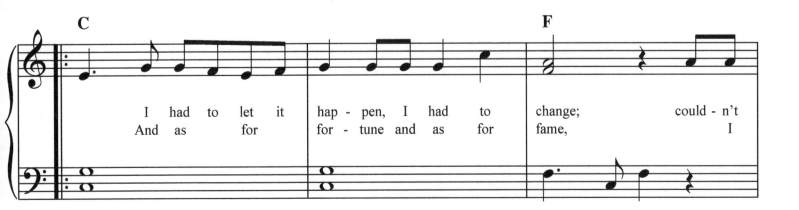

**C**                                                **F**

I   had   to   let   it    hap - pen, I   had   to     change;         could - n't
And   as    for      for - tune and   as   for     fame,           I

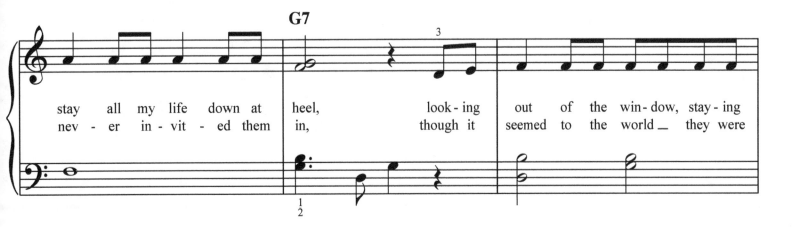

                            **G7**

stay   all   my   life   down   at    heel,         look - ing    out   of   the   win - dow, stay - ing
nev - er   in - vit - ed them   in,        though it    seemed   to   the   world __ they were

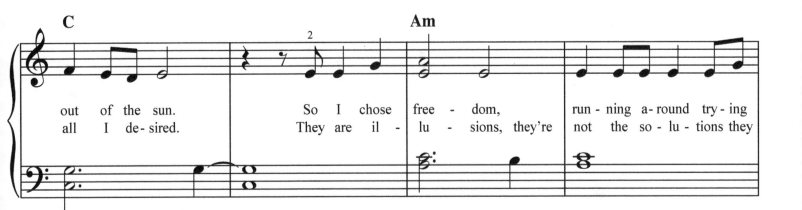

**C**                                      **Am**

out   of   the   sun.         So   I   chose   free - dom,      run - ning a - round try - ing
all   I   de - sired.       They are   il - lu - sions, they're    not   the   so - lu - tions they

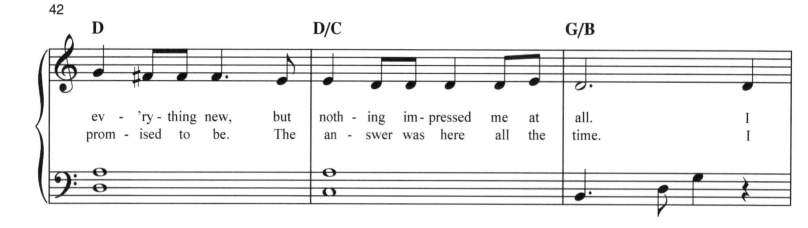

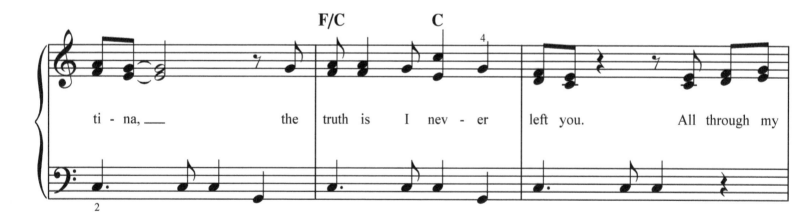

**F**

dis - tance. _____

Have I said too much? There's

**Em7**

noth - ing more I can think of to say to you.

But

**Fmaj7**

**C**

**D.S. al Coda**

all you have to do is look at me to know that ev - 'ry word is true.

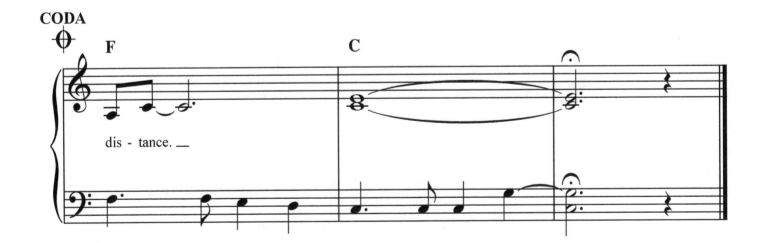

**CODA**

**F**

**C**

dis - tance. _____

# EVERYTHING'S COMING UP ROSES

## from GYPSY

Lyrics by STEPHEN SONDHEIM
Music by JULE STYNE

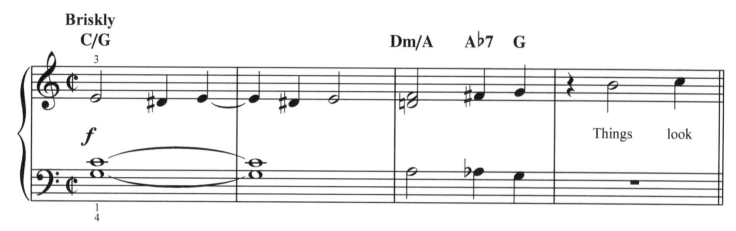

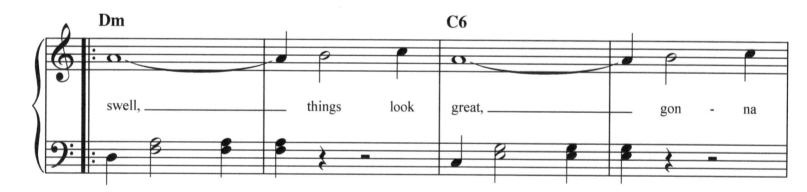

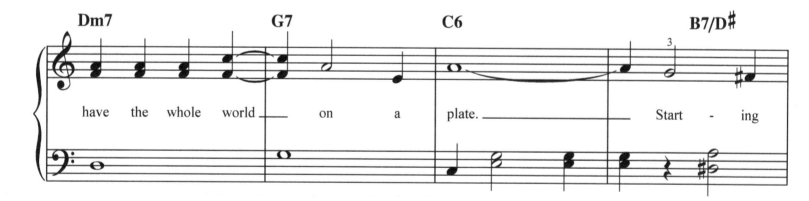

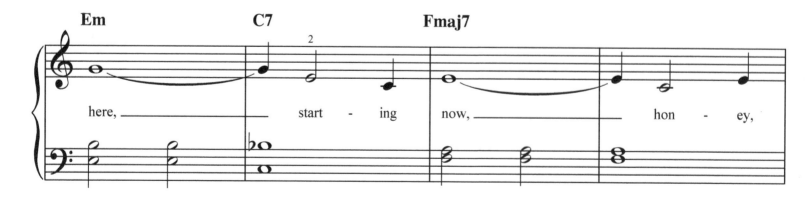

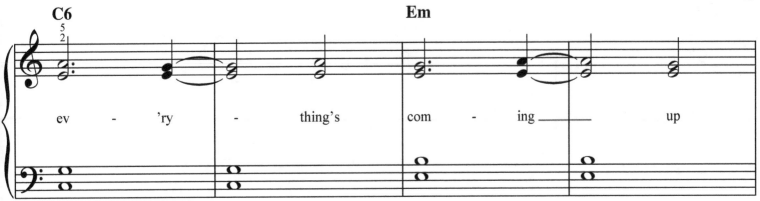

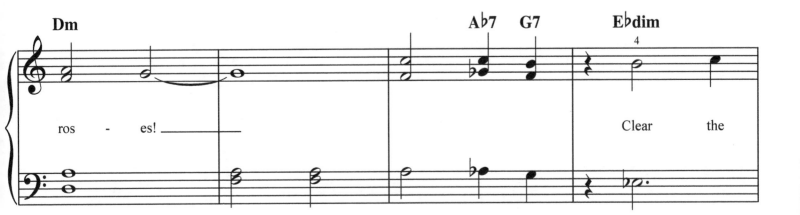

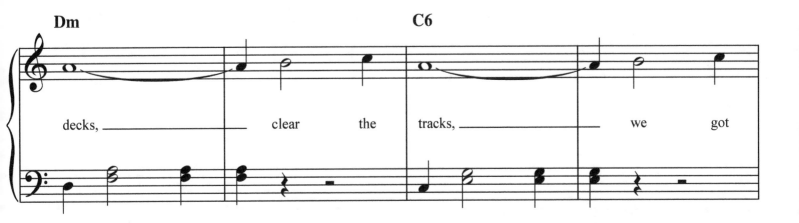

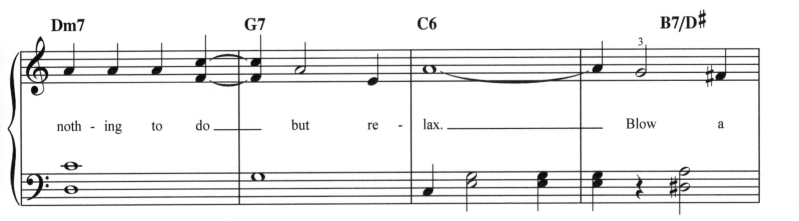

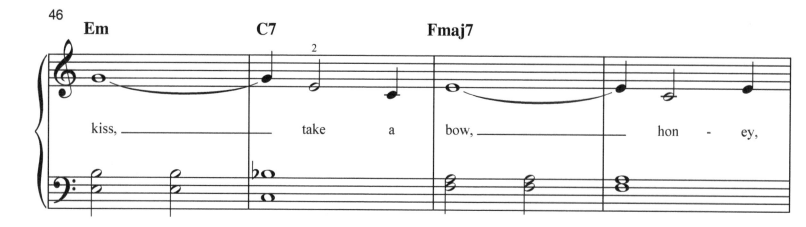

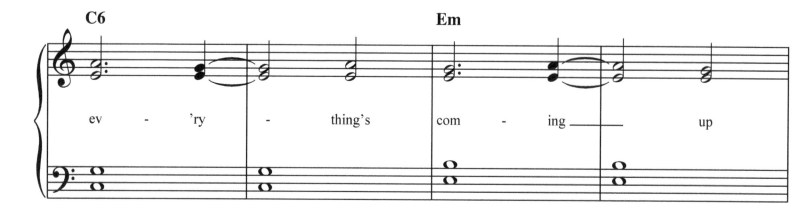

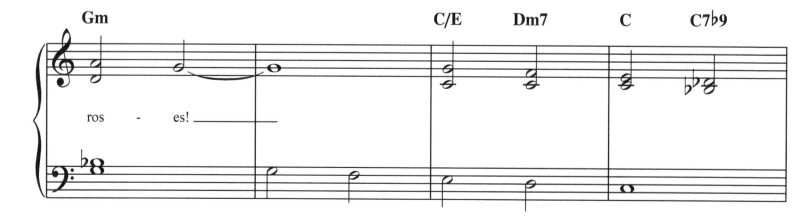

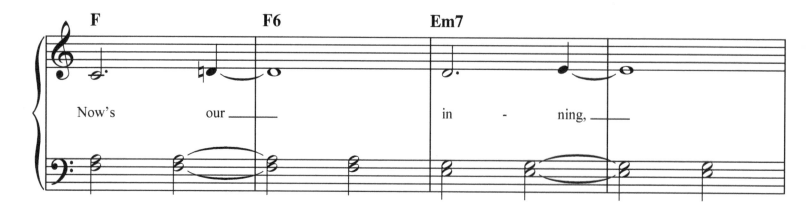

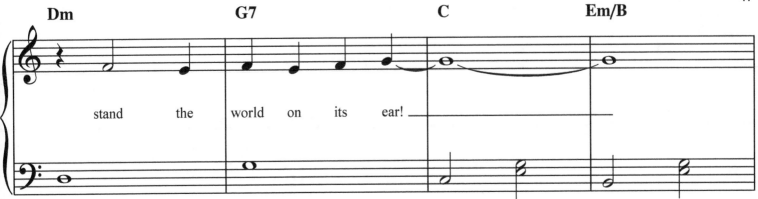

stand the world on its ear! ___

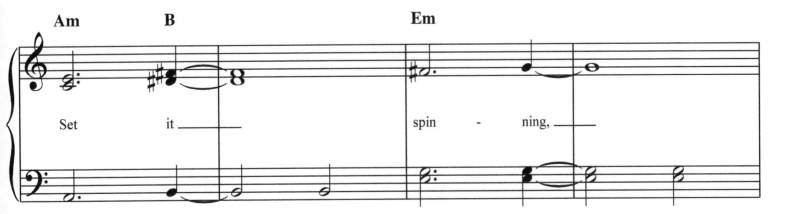

Set it ___ spin - ning, ___

that - 'll be just the be - gin - ning! ___ Cur - tain

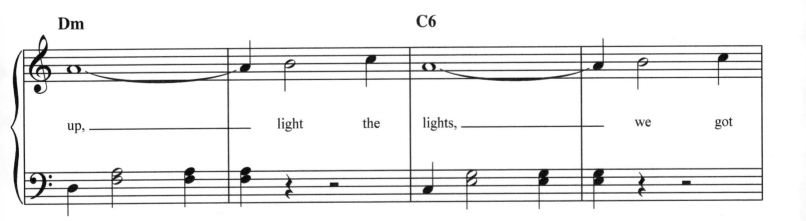

up, ___ light the lights, ___ we got

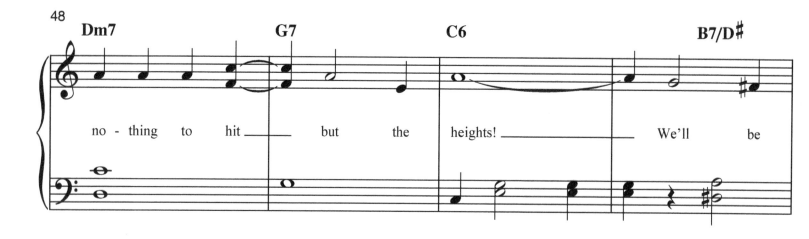

**Dm7**     **G7**     **C6**     **B7/D#**

no - thing to hit \_\_\_\_ but the heights! _____ We'll be

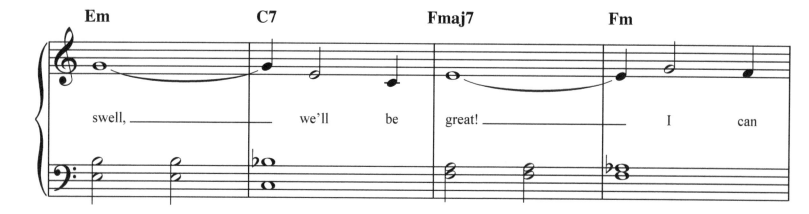

**Em**     **C7**     **Fmaj7**     **Fm**

swell, _____ we'll be great! _____ I can

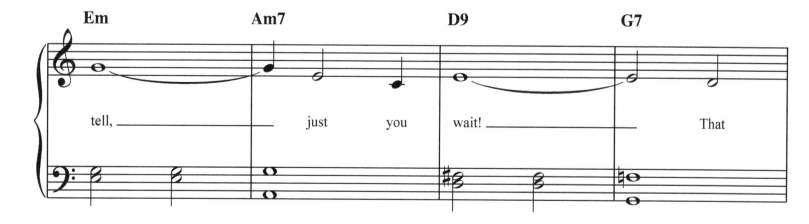

**Em**     **Am7**     **D9**     **G7**

tell, _____ just you wait! _____ That

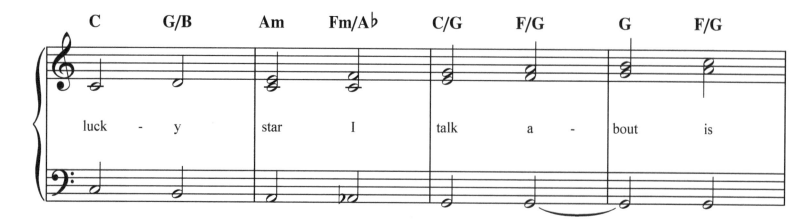

**C**   **G/B**   **Am**   **Fm/Ab**   **C/G**   **F/G**   **G**   **F/G**

luck - y star I talk a - bout is

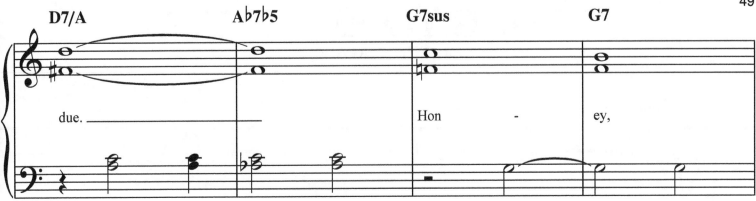

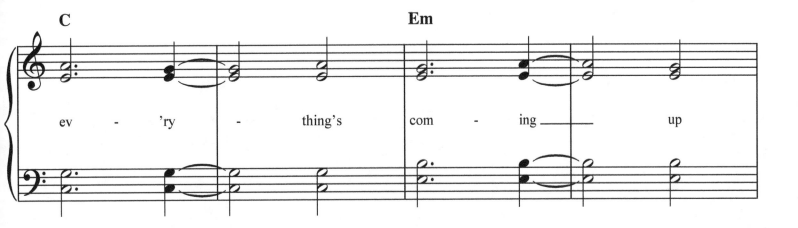

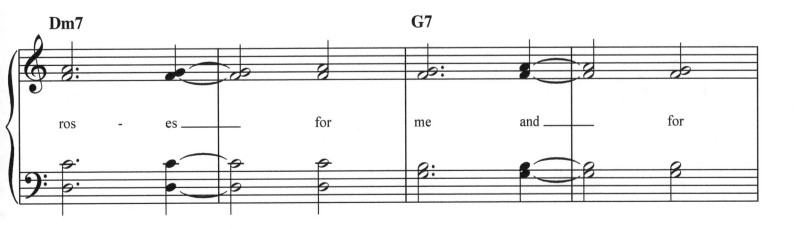

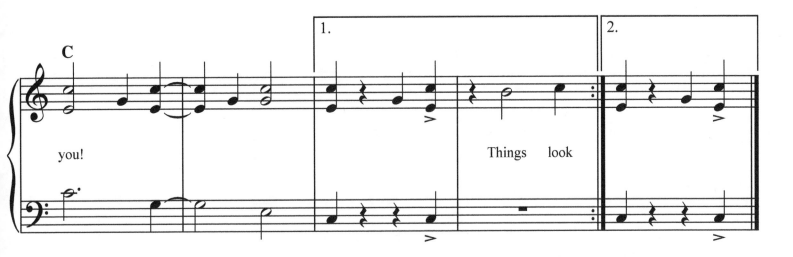

# GETTING TO KNOW YOU

## from THE KING AND I

Lyrics by OSCAR HAMMERSTEIN II
Music by RICHARD RODGERS

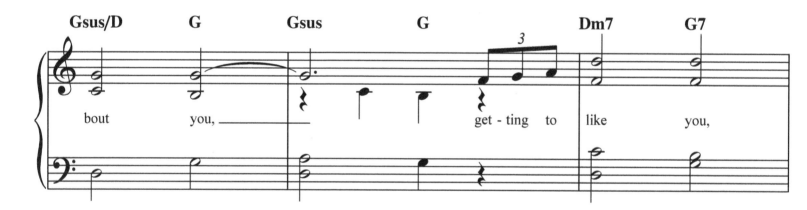

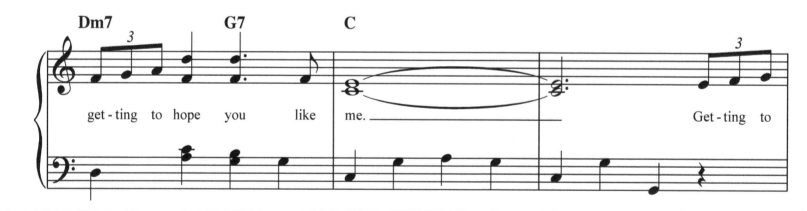

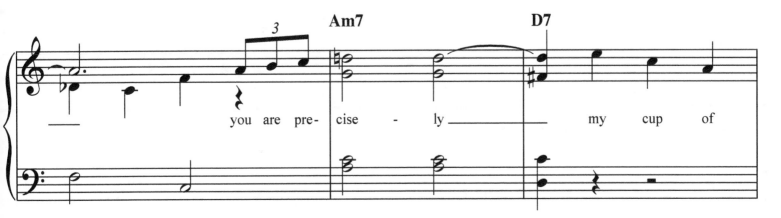

you are pre- cise - ly _____ my cup of

tea! Get - ting to know you,

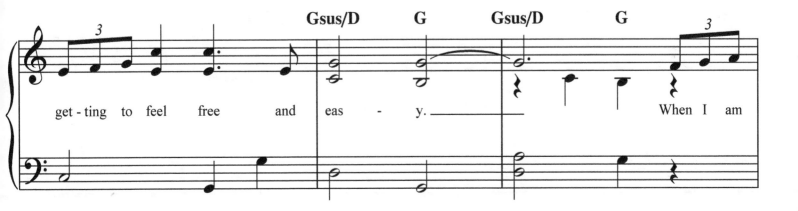

get - ting to feel free and eas - y. _____ When I am

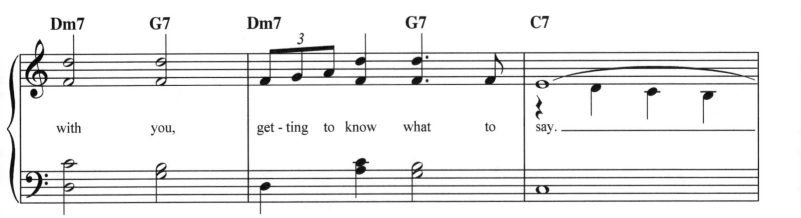

with you, get - ting to know what to say. _____

Have-n't you no - ticed? Sud-den-ly I'm bright and

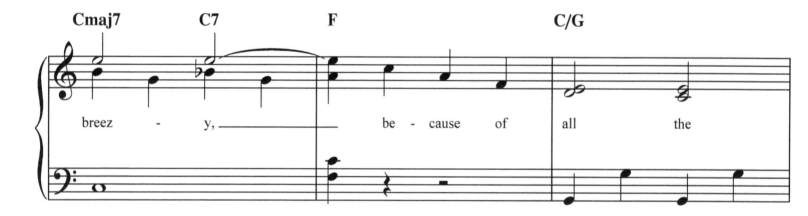

breez - y, _____ be - cause of all the

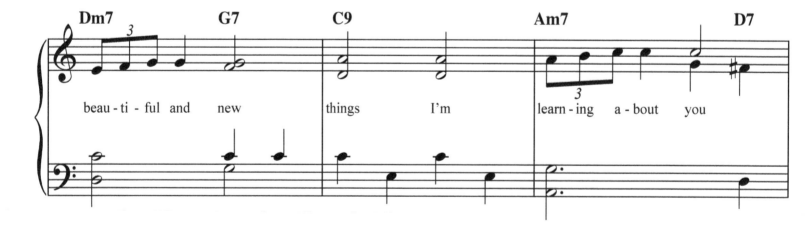

beau-ti-ful and new things I'm learn-ing a-bout you

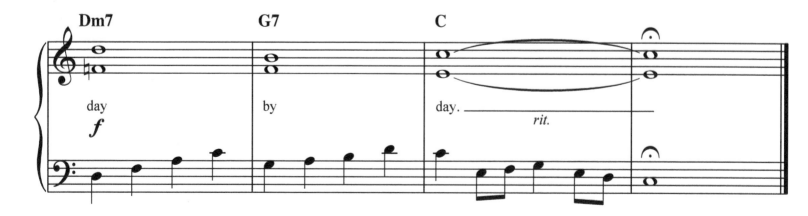

day by day. _____

# HELLO, DOLLY!
## from HELLO, DOLLY!

Music and Lyric by
JERRY HERMAN

Medium Strut tempo

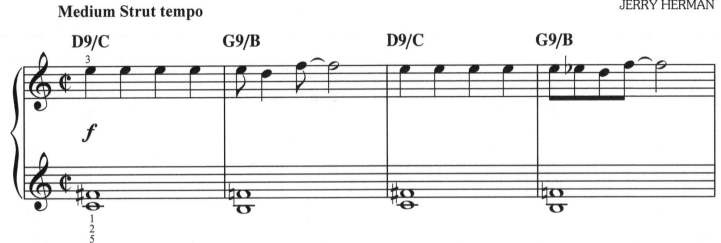

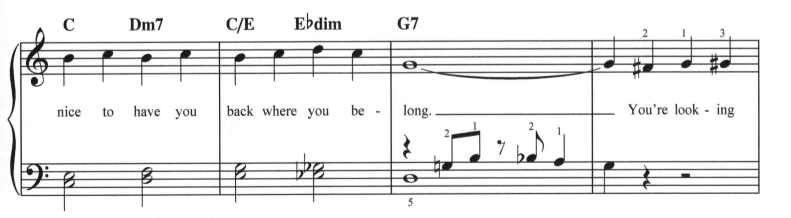

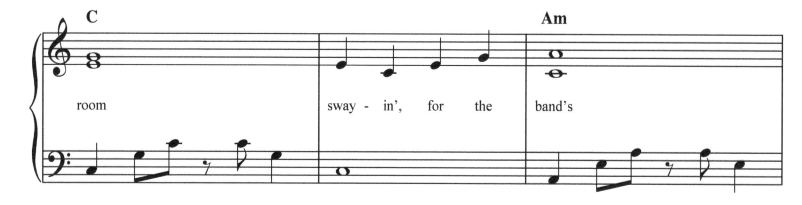

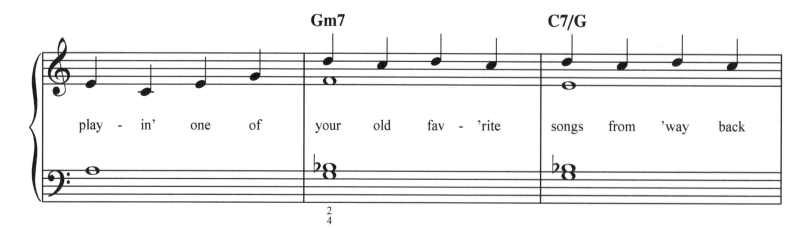

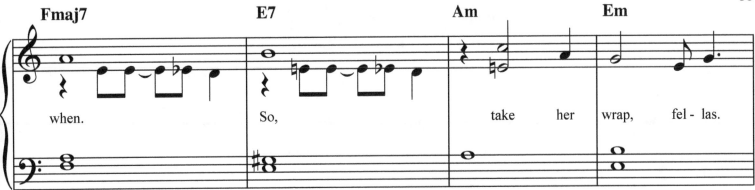

when. So, take her wrap, fel - las.

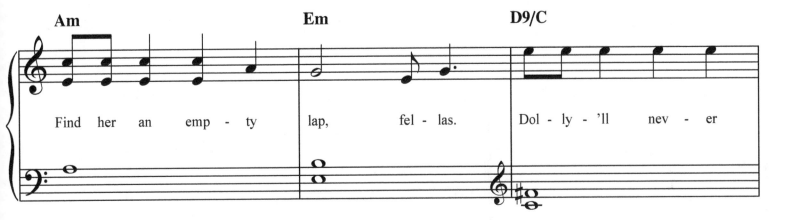

Find her an emp - ty lap, fel - las. Dol - ly - 'll nev - er

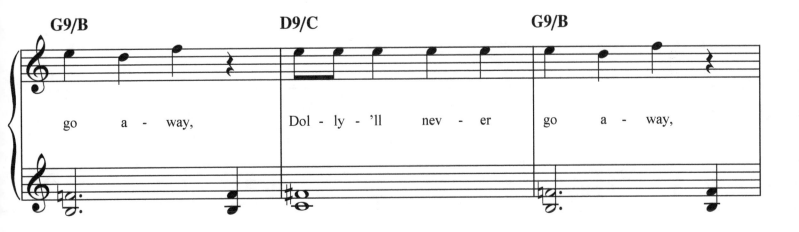

go a - way, Dol - ly - 'll nev - er go a - way,

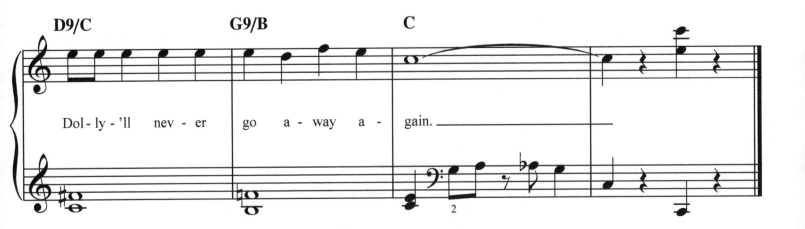

Dol - ly - 'll nev - er go a - way a - gain. _____

# HEY THERE
## from THE PAJAMA GAME

Words and Music by RICHARD ADLER
and JERRY ROSS

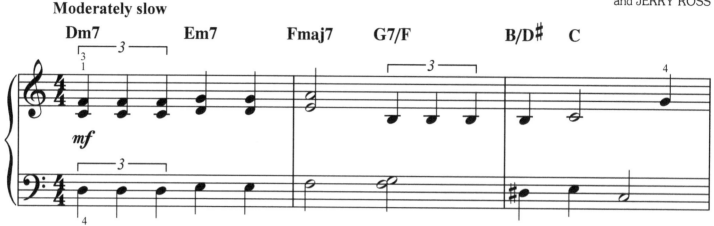

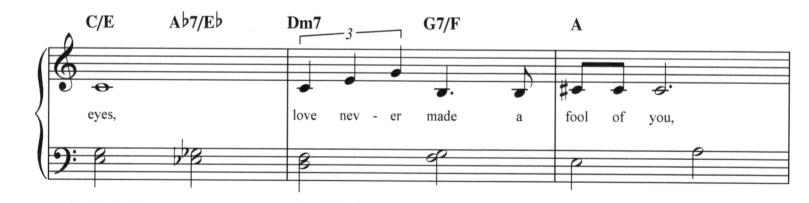

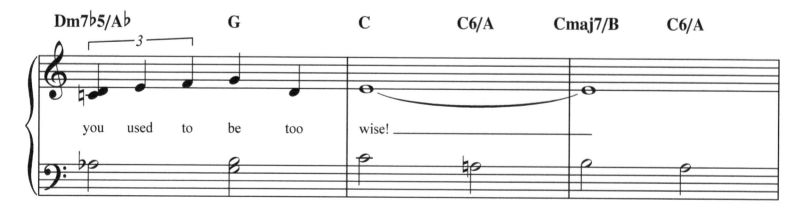

Hey there, _____ you on that high fly - ing cloud,

though she won't throw a crumb to you, you think some - day she'll come to you;

bet - ter for - get her, _____ her with her nose in the air,

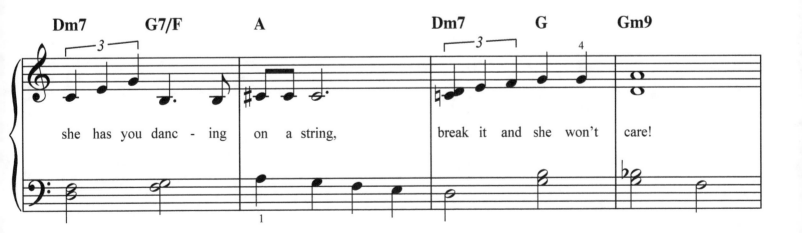

she has you danc - ing on a string, break it and she won't care!

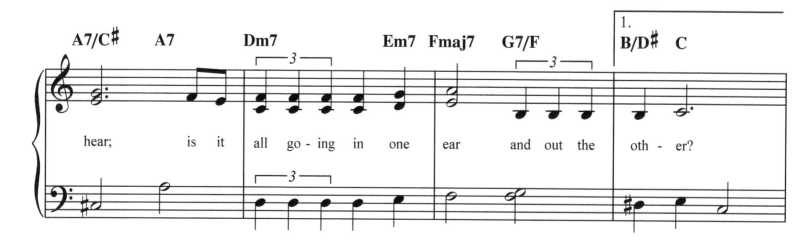

# HOW ARE THINGS
# IN GLOCCA MORRA
**from FINIAN'S RAINBOW**

Words by E.Y. "YIP" HARBURG
Music by BURTON LANE

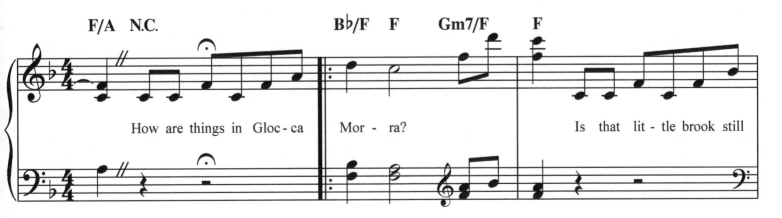

Mor - ra? Is that wil - low tree still weep - ing there?

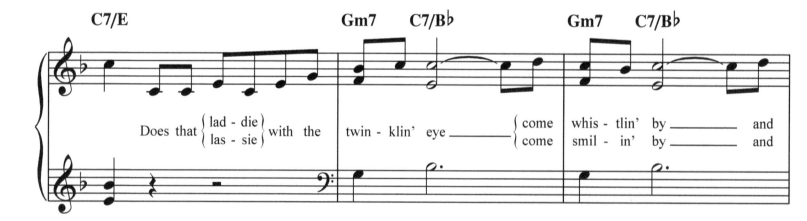

Does that {lad - die / las - sie} with the twin - klin' eye {come whis - tlin' by _____ and / come smil - in' by _____ and

does he walk a - way / does she walk a - way} sad and dream - y there, not to see me there?

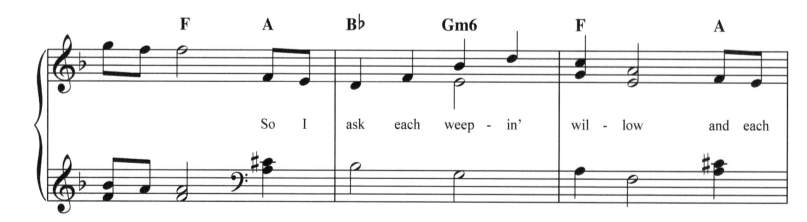

So I ask each weep - in' wil - low and each

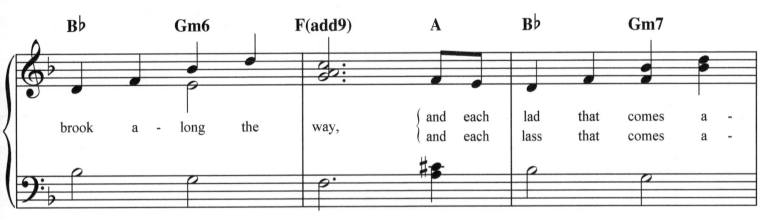

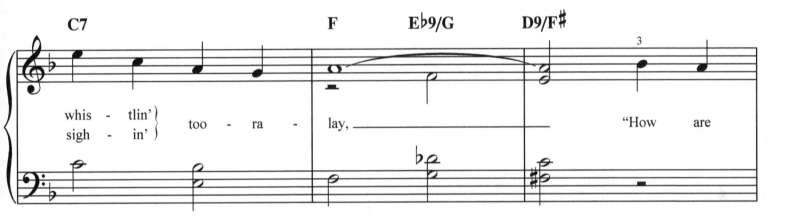

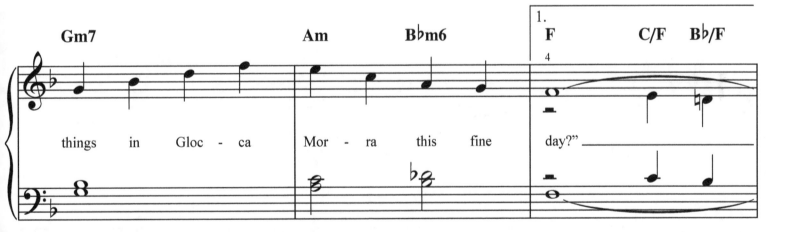

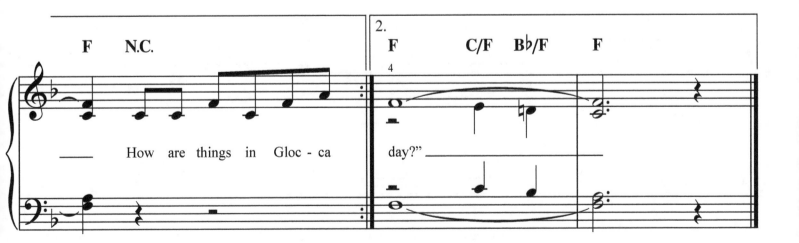

# I COULD HAVE DANCED ALL NIGHT

**from MY FAIR LADY**

Words by ALAN JAY LERNER
Music by FREDERICK LOEWE

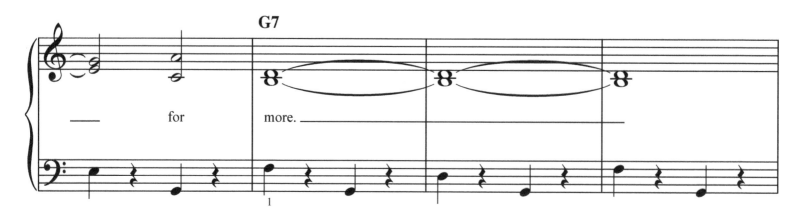

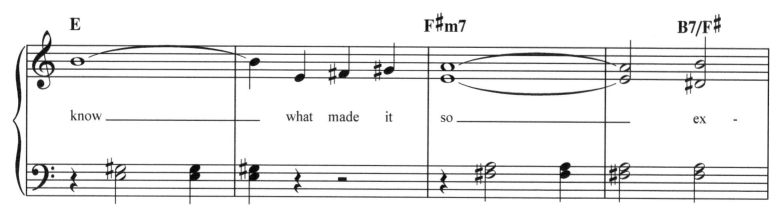

know _____ when he _____ be - gan to

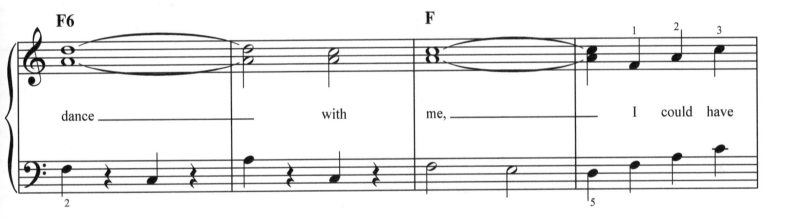

dance _____ with me, _____ I could have

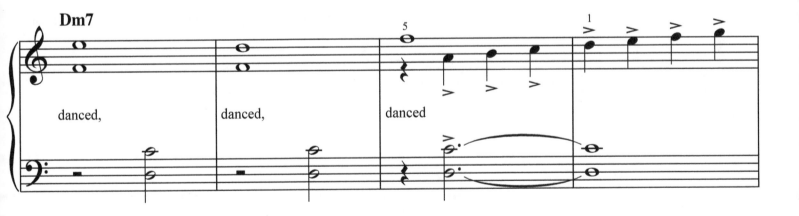

danced, danced, danced

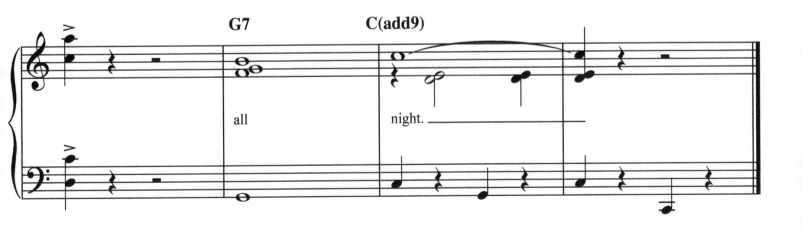

all night. _____

# I DON'T KNOW HOW TO LOVE HIM

**from JESUS CHRIST SUPERSTAR**

Words by TIM RICE
Music by ANDREW LLOYD WEBBER

**Slowly and tenderly**

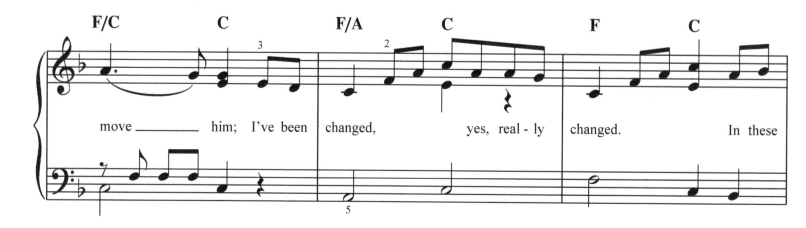

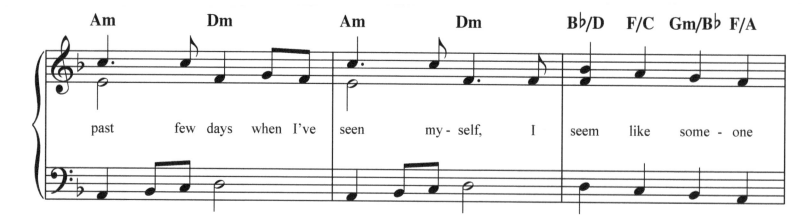

else. I don't know how to take _____ this,

I don't see why he moves _____ me. He's a man, he's just a

man, and I've had so man - y men be - fore in

ver - y man - y ways. _____ He's just one more.

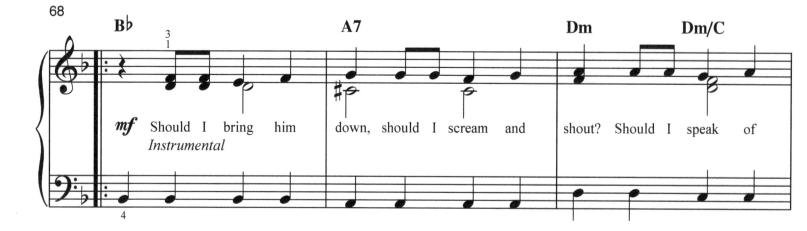

Should I bring him down, should I scream and shout? Should I speak of
*Instrumental*

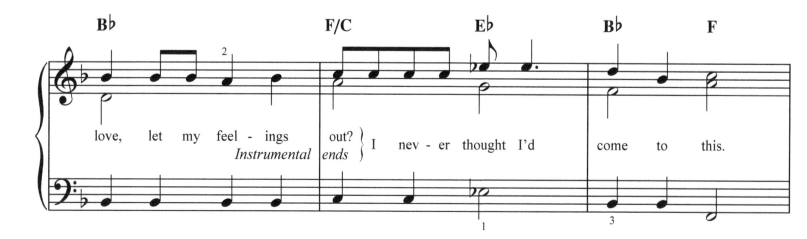

love, let my feel - ings out?
*Instrumental ends* } I nev - er thought I'd come to this.

What's it all a - bout?

Don't you think it's rath - er fun - ny I should be in this po -
Yet ___ if he said he loved ___ me, I'd be lost, ___ I'd be

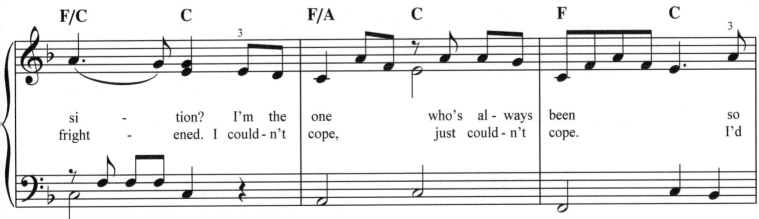

si - tion? I'm the one who's al - ways been so
fright - ened. I could - n't cope, just could - n't cope. I'd

calm, so cool, no lov - er's fool, run - ning ev - 'ry ___
turn my head, I'd back a - way, I would - n't want to ___

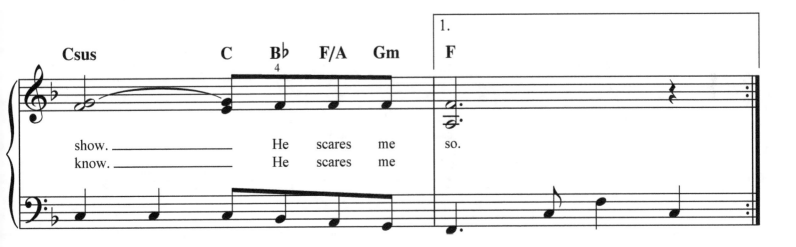

1.

show. ___ He scares me so.
know. ___ He scares me

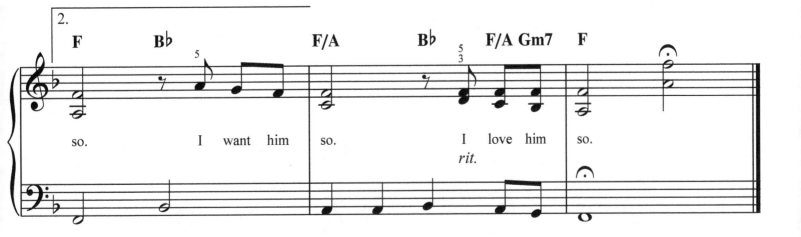

2.

so. I want him so. I love him so.
*rit.*

# I DREAMED A DREAM

## from LES MISÉRABLES

Music by CLAUDE-MICHEL SCHÖNBERG
Lyrics by ALAIN BOUBLIL, JEAN-MARC NATEL
and HERBERT KRETZMER

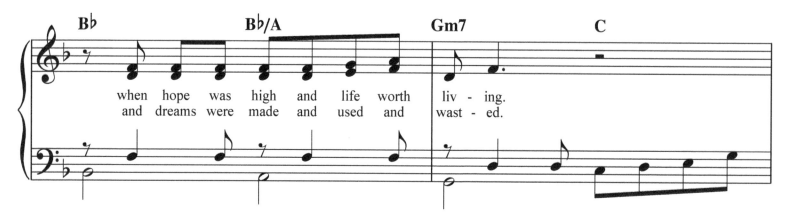

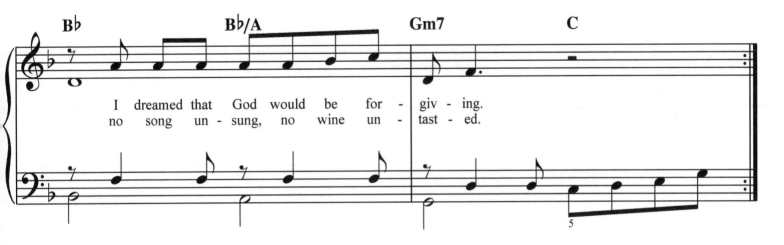

I dreamed that God would be for-giv-ing.
no song un-sung, no wine un-tast-ed.

But the ti-gers come at night with their voic-es soft as

thun-der, _____ as they tear your hope a-part,

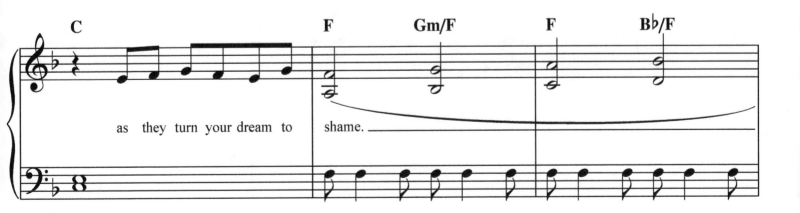

as they turn your dream to shame. _____

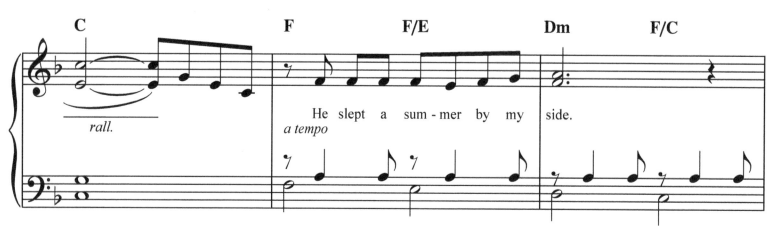

He slept a sum-mer by my side.

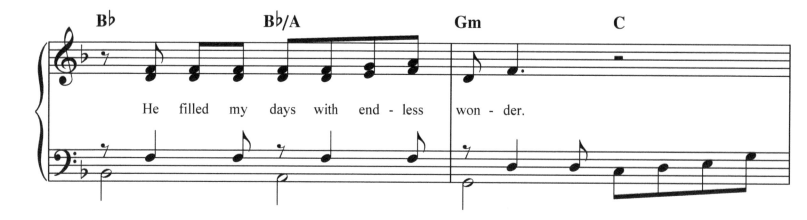

He filled my days with end-less won-der.

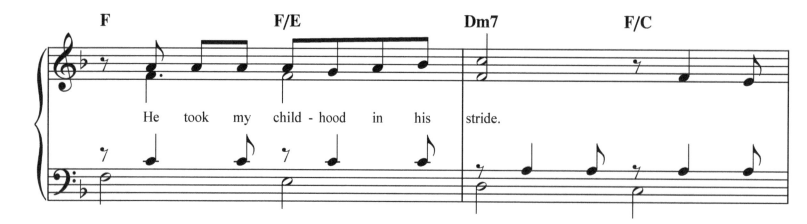

He took my child-hood in his stride.

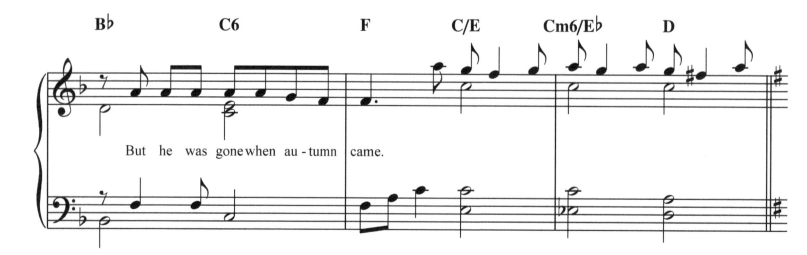

But he was gone when au-tumn came.

And still I dreamed he'd come to me,

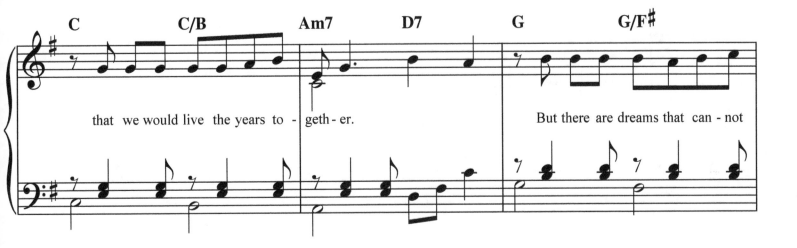

that we would live the years to - geth - er. But there are dreams that can - not

be, and there are storms we can - not weath - er.

I had a dream my life would

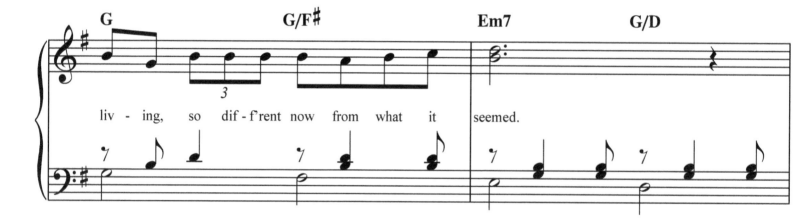

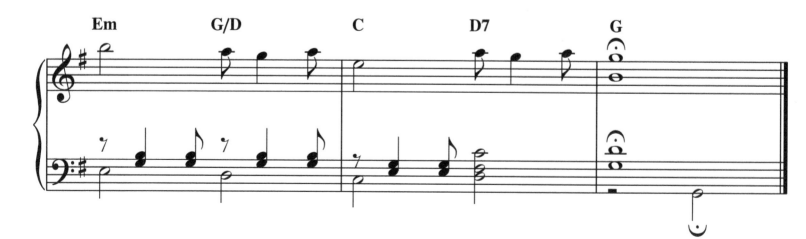

# I'M GONNA WASH THAT MAN RIGHT OUTA MY HAIR

from SOUTH PACIFIC

Lyrics by OSCAR HAMMERSTEIN II
Music by RICHARD RODGERS

Moderate Swing

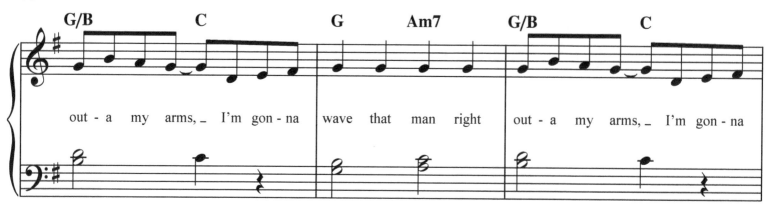

out - a my arms, _ I'm gon - na wave that man right out - a my arms, _ I'm gon - na

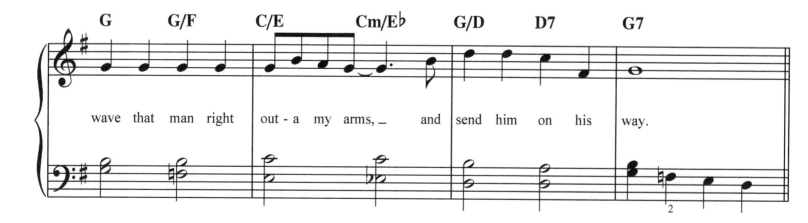

wave that man right out - a my arms, _ and send him on his way.

Don't try to patch it up, tear it up, tear it up! Wash him out, dry him out,

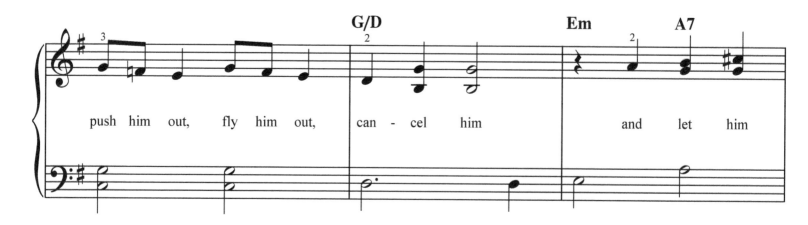

push him out, fly him out, can - cel him and let him

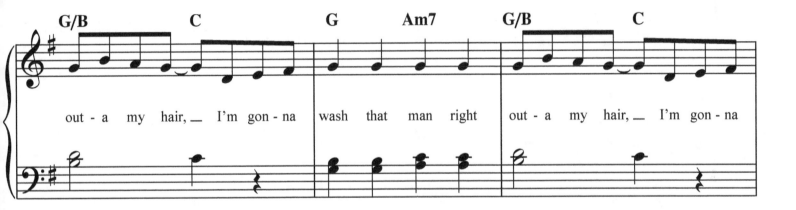

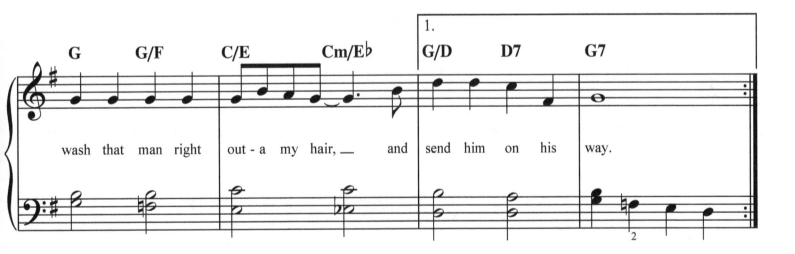

# I GOT PLENTY O' NUTTIN'

### from PORGY AND BESS®

Music and Lyrics by GEORGE GERSHWIN,
DuBOSE and DOROTHY HEYWARD and IRA GERSHWIN

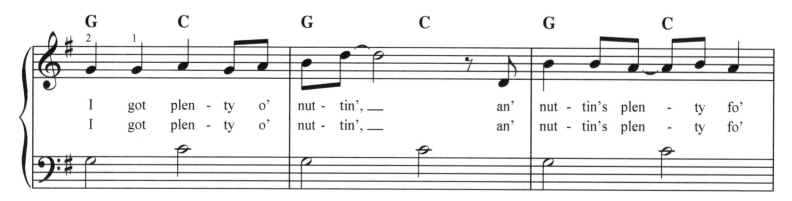

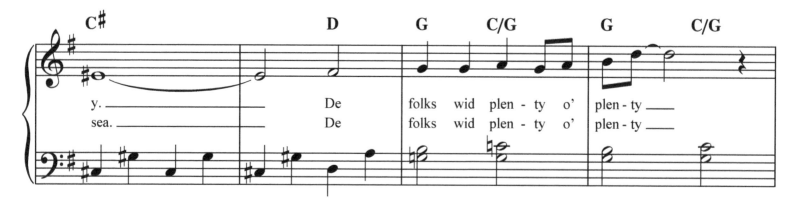

got a lock ___ on de door, _____
got to pray ___ all de day. _____
'fraid some - bod - y's a -
Seems wid plen - ty you

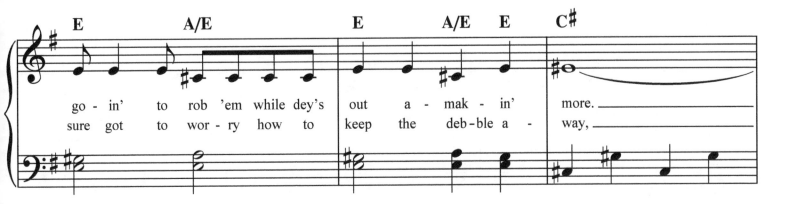

go - in' to rob 'em while dey's out a - mak - in' more. _____
sure got to wor - ry how to keep the deb - ble a - way, _____

___ What a - for? _____
___ a - way. _____

I got no lock on de door, dat's no way to be. _____
I ain't a fret - tin' 'bout ___ hell 'til de time ar - rive. _____

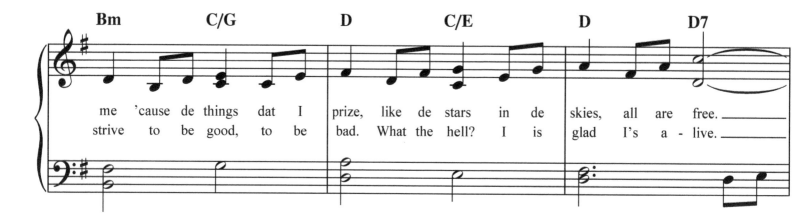

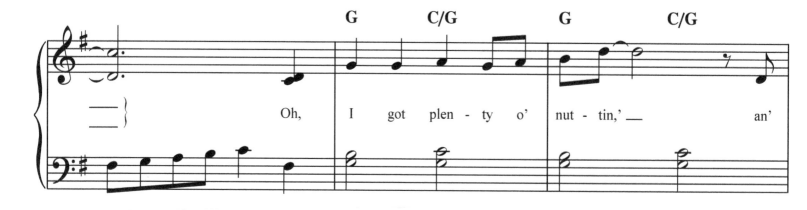

heb - ben the whole day long. No use com - plain - in'! Got my

gal, _____ got my Lawd, _____ got my

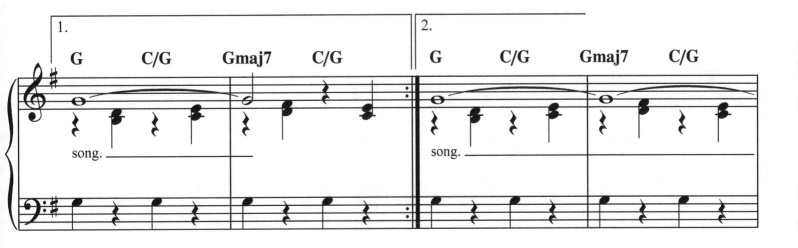

song. _____ song. _____

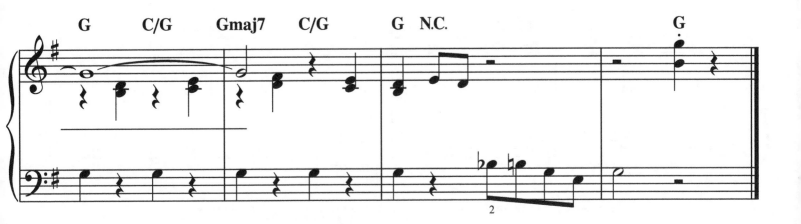

# I LOVE PARIS

## from CAN-CAN

Words and Music by
COLE PORTER

**Slow Fox-trot tempo**

I love Par-is in the spring-time, _____

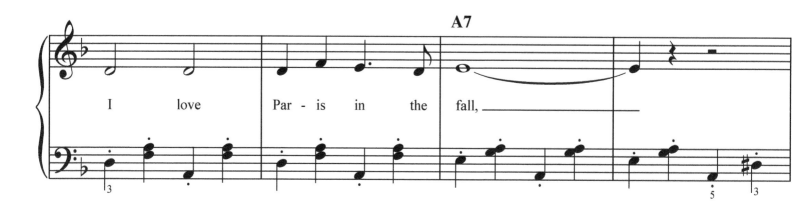

I love Par-is in the fall, _____

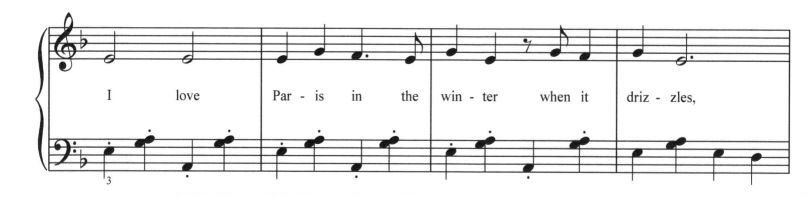

I love Par-is in the win-ter when it driz-zles,

I love Par-is in the sum-mer, when it siz-zles.

I love Par - is ev - 'ry mo - ment, _____

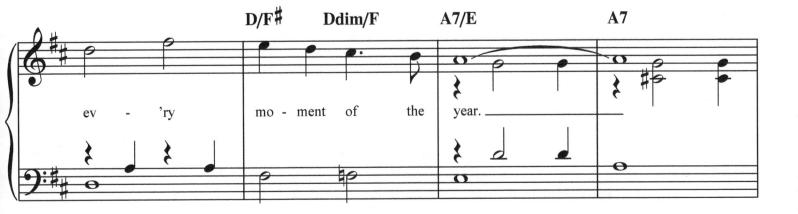

D/F♯    Ddim/F        A7/E              A7

ev - 'ry    mo - ment of the    year. _____

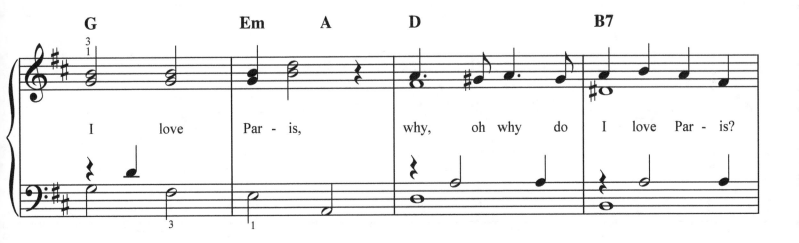

G            Em      A        D                B7

I love    Par - is,    why, oh why do    I love Par - is?

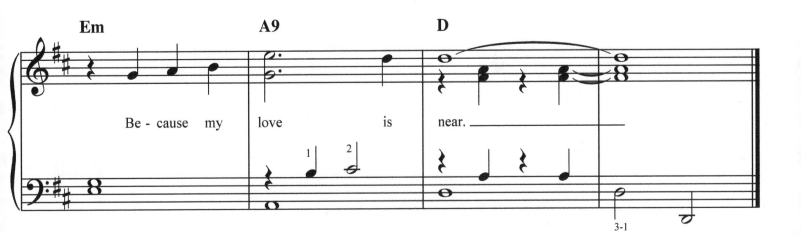

Em                    A9              D

Be - cause my    love    is    near. _____

# I WHISTLE A HAPPY TUNE

### from THE KING AND I

Lyrics by OSCAR HAMMERSTEIN II
Music by RICHARD RODGERS

Moderately

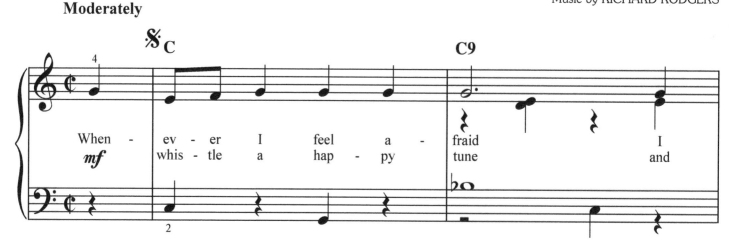

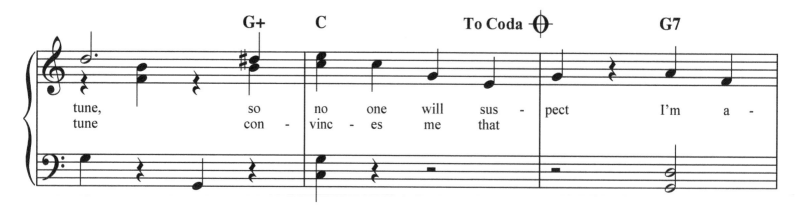

strike a care - less pose _____ and whis - tle a hap - py

tune _____ and no one ev - er knows I'm a - fraid. _____

_____ The re - sult of this de - cep - tion is

ver - y strange to _____ tell, for when I fool the

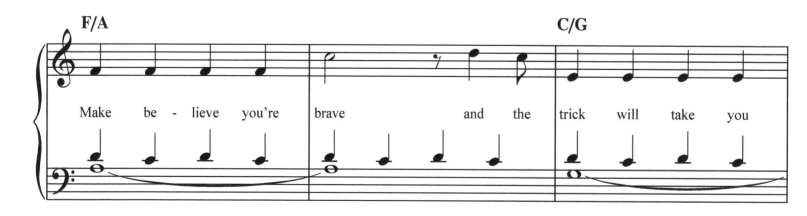

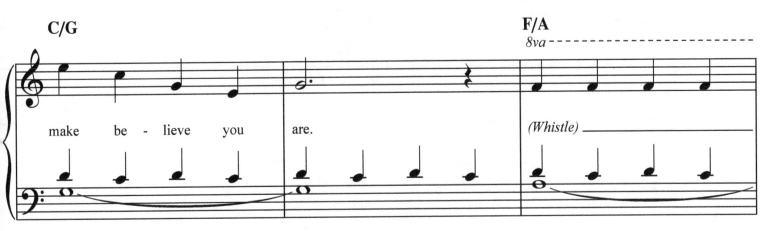

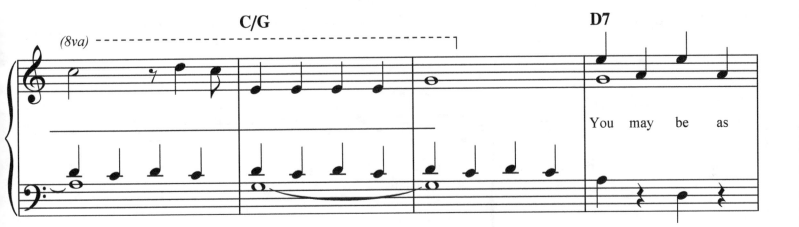

# I'VE GROWN ACCUSTOMED TO HER FACE

**from MY FAIR LADY**

Words by ALAN JAY LERNER
Music by FREDERICK LOEWE

I've grown ac- / cus-tomed to her face; ____ she al-most
cus-tomed to her face; ____ she al-most

makes the day be - gin. / I've grown ac -
makes the day be - gin. / I've got - ten

cus - tomed to the tune she / whis - tles night and noon; her
used to hear her tune say "Good / morn - ing" ev - 'ry day; her

smiles, her frowns, her ups, her downs are sec - ond
joys, her woes, her highs, her lows are sec - ond

na - ture to me now, _____ like breath - ing
na - ture to me now, _____ like breath - ing

*mp*

out and breath - ing in. I was se -
out and breath - ing in. I'm ver - y

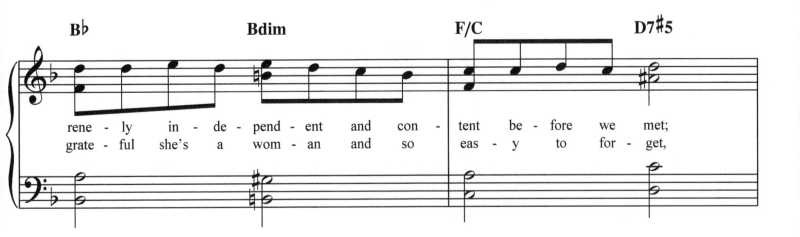

rene - ly in - de - pend - ent and con - tent be - fore we met;
grate - ful she's a wom - an and so eas - y to for - get,

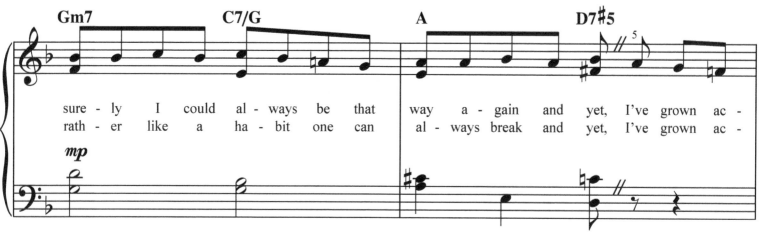

surely I could always be that way again and yet, I've grown ac-
rath-er like a ha-bit one can always break and yet, I've grown ac-

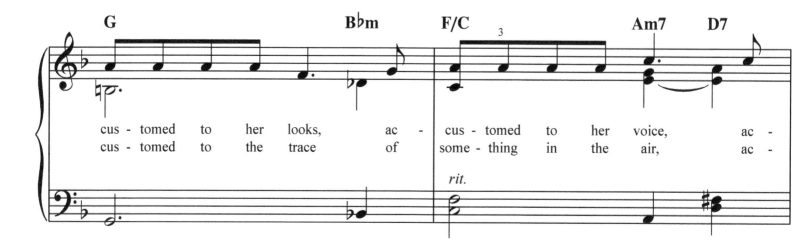

cus-tomed to her looks, ac-cus-tomed to her voice, ac-
cus-tomed to the trace of some-thing in the air, ac-

*rit.*

cus-tomed to her face.
cus-tomed to her

I've grown ac-
*a tempo*

face.
*a tempo*

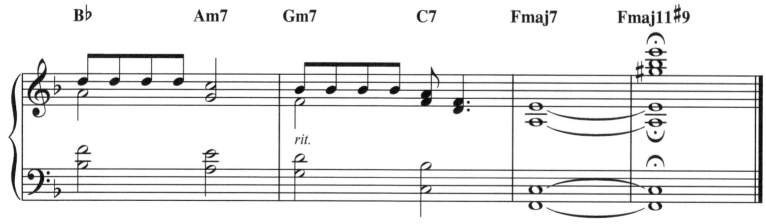

*rit.*

# IF I LOVED YOU
## from CAROUSEL

Lyrics by OSCAR HAMMERSTEIN II
Music by RICHARD RODGERS

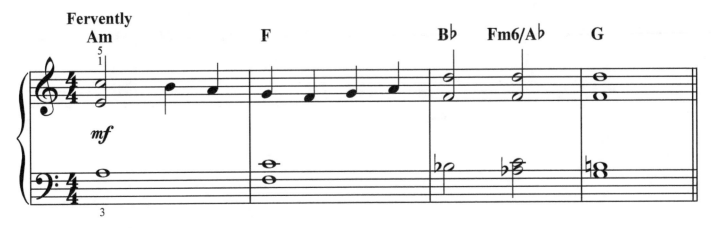

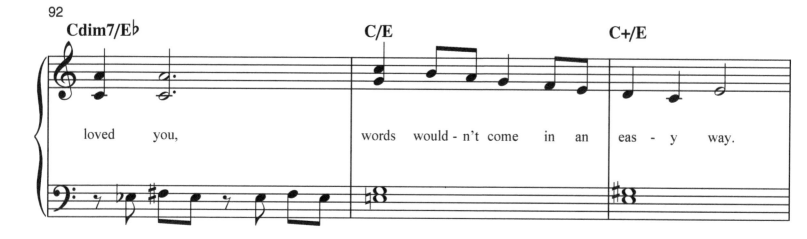

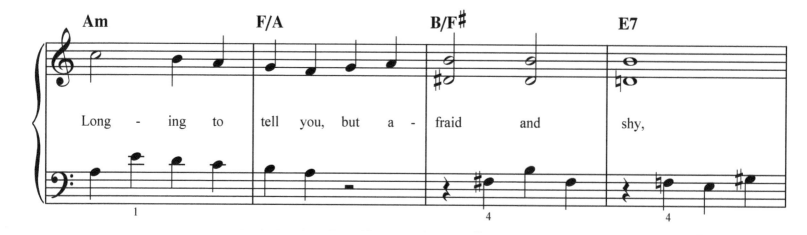

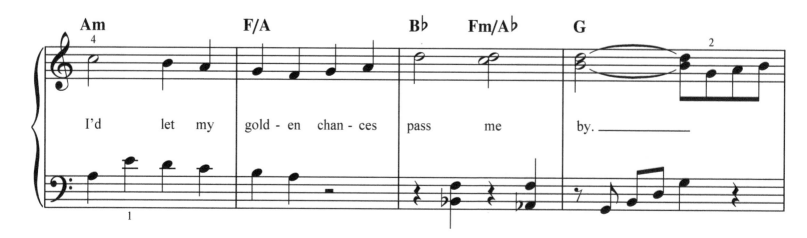

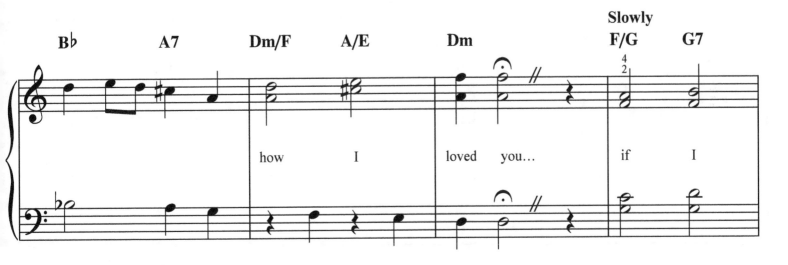

# IF I WERE A BELL
## from GUYS AND DOLLS

By FRANK LOESSER

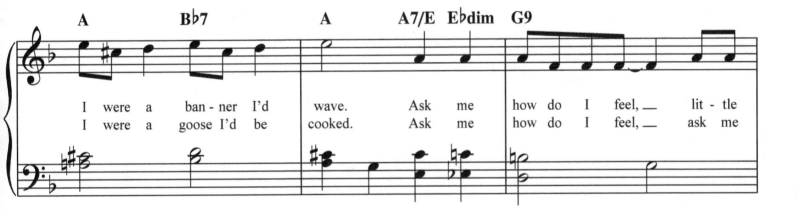

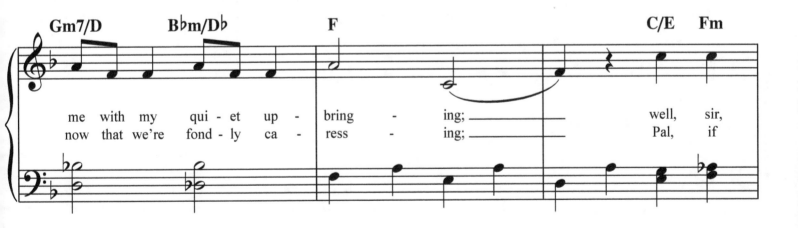

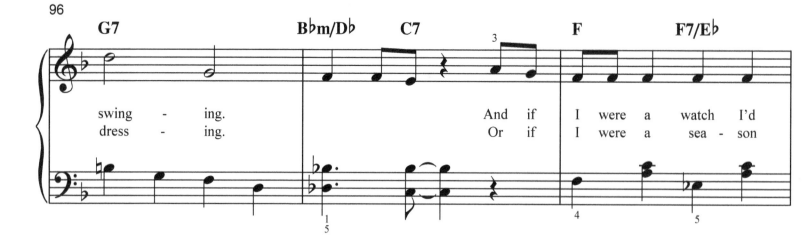

**G7** swing - ing. / dress - ing. **B♭m/D♭** **C7** And if / Or if **F** I were a watch I'd / I were a sea - son **F7/E♭**

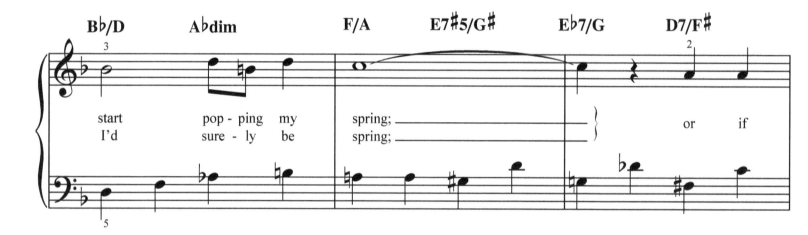

**B♭/D** start / I'd **A♭dim** pop - ping my / sure - ly be **F/A** spring; **E7♯5/G♯** spring; **E♭7/G** **D7/F♯** or if

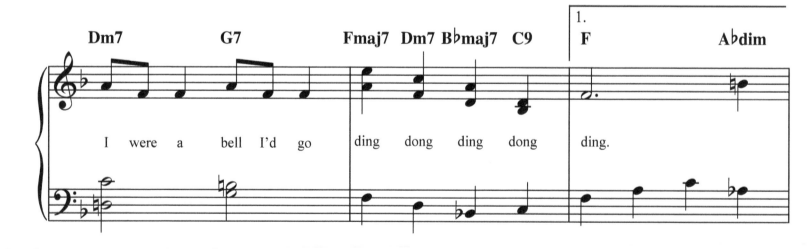

**Dm7** I were a **G7** bell I'd go **Fmaj7 Dm7 B♭maj7 C9** ding dong ding dong **1.** **F** ding. **A♭dim**

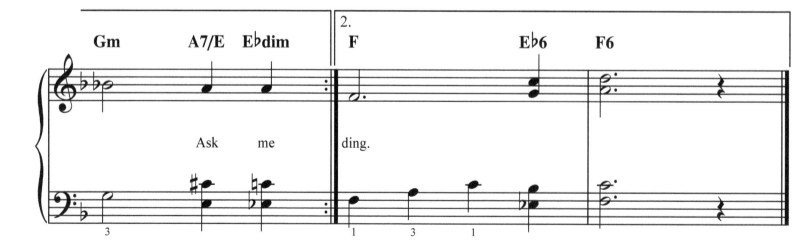

**Gm** **A7/E E♭dim** Ask me **2.** **F** ding. **E♭6** **F6**

# MAME
## from MAME

Music and Lyric by
JERRY HERMAN

**Moderately, with a lilt**

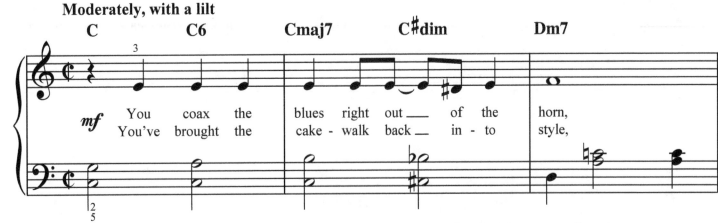

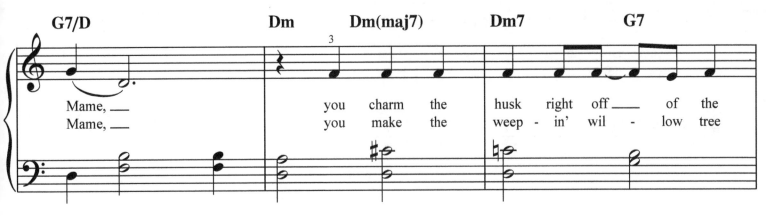

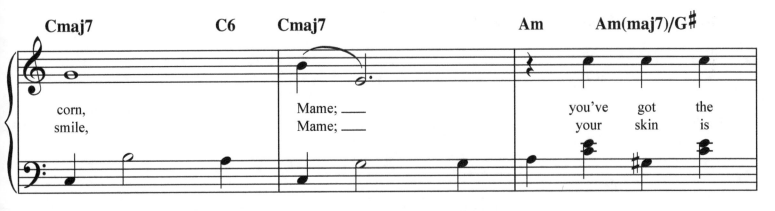

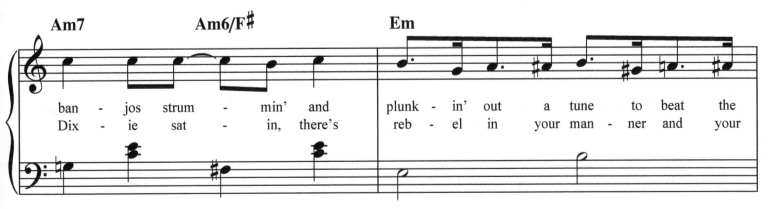

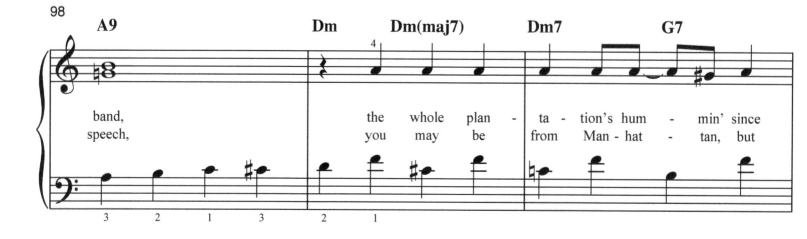

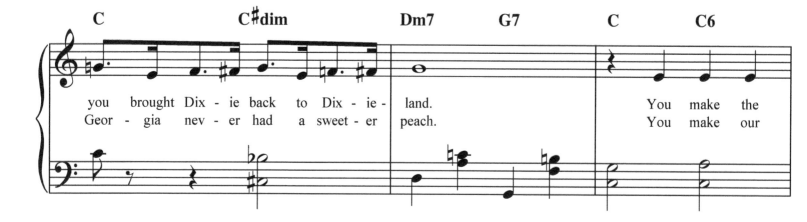

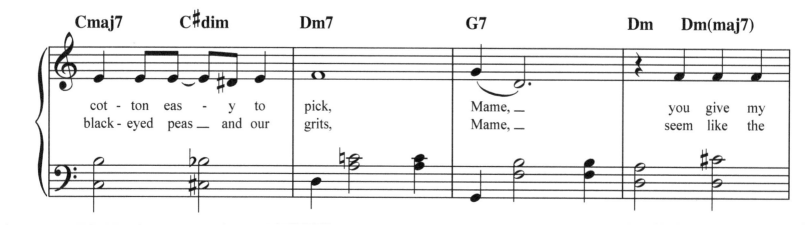

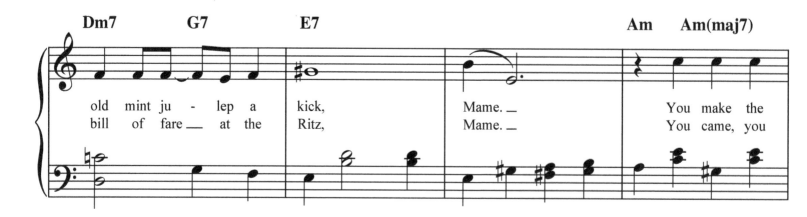

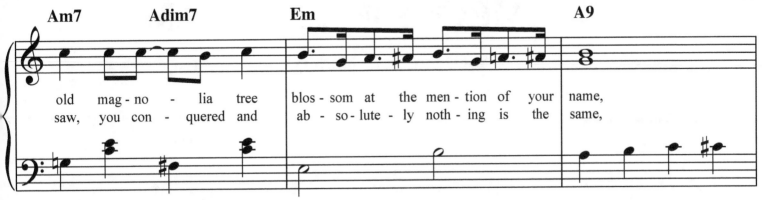

old mag - no - lia tree blos - som at the men - tion of your name,
saw, you con - quered and ab - so - lute - ly noth - ing is the same,

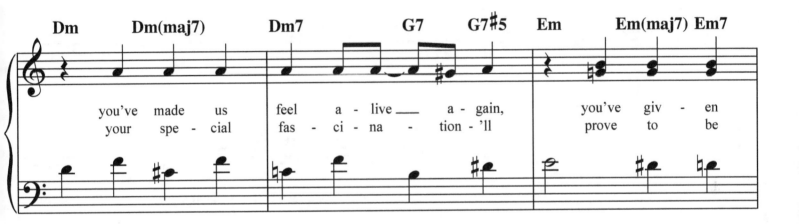

you've made us feel a - live __ a - gain, you've giv - en
your spe - cial fas - ci - na - tion - 'll prove to be

us the drive __ a - gain, to make the South re - vive __ a - gain,
in - spi - ra - tion - al, we think you're just sen - sa - tion - al,

Mame.

Mame.

# THE IMPOSSIBLE DREAM
### (The Quest)
#### from MAN OF LA MANCHA

Lyric by JOE DARION
Music by MITCH LEIGH

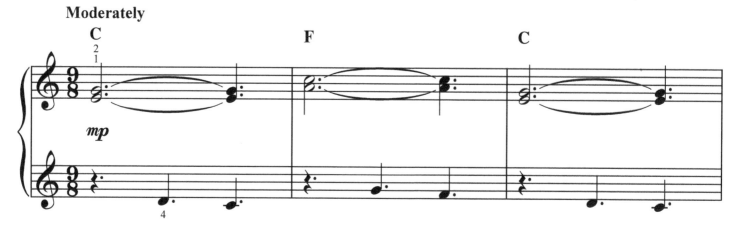

right _____ the un-right-a - ble wrong, _____ to love _____ pure and chaste from a -

far, _____ to try _____ when your arms are too wear - y, _____ to

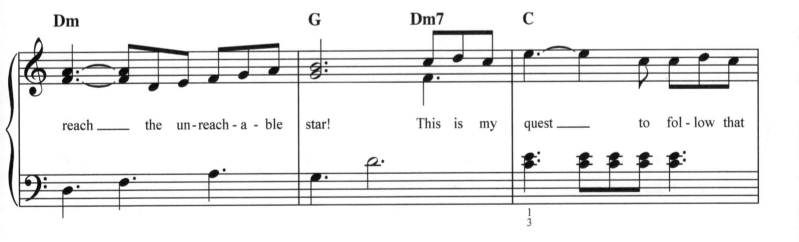

reach _____ the un-reach-a - ble star! This is my quest _____ to fol - low that

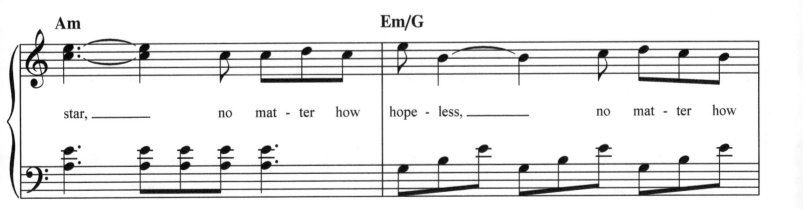

star, _____ no mat - ter how hope - less, _____ no mat - ter how

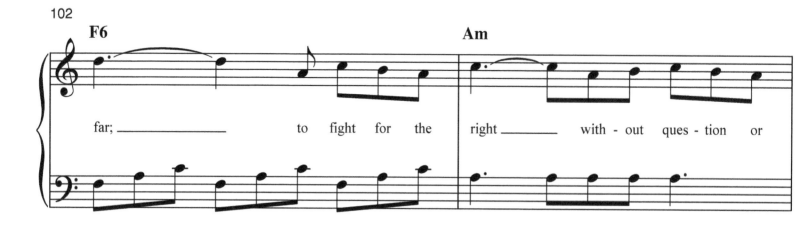

far; _____ to fight for the right _____ with - out ques - tion or

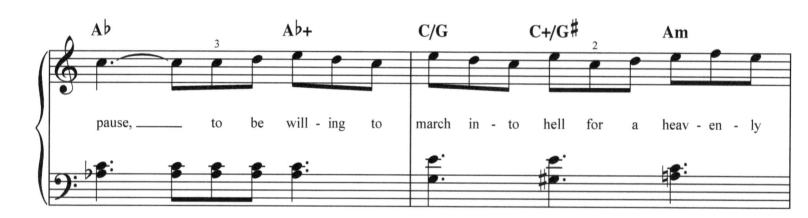

pause, _____ to be will - ing to march in - to hell for a heav - en - ly

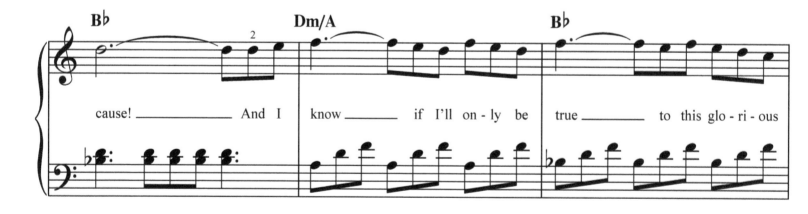

cause! _____ And I know _____ if I'll on - ly be true _____ to this glo - ri - ous

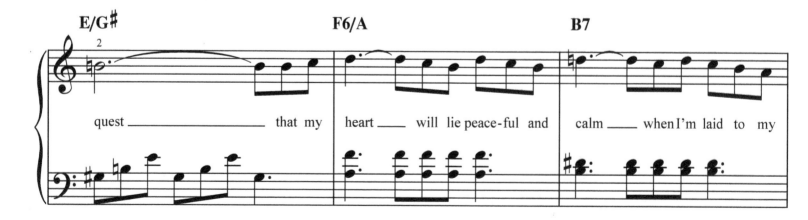

quest _____ that my heart \_\_\_ will lie peace-ful and calm \_\_\_ when I'm laid to my

rest. *rit.* And the world ___ will be bet-ter for this: ___ that one

*a tempo*

man, ___ scorned and cov-ered with scars, ___ still ___ strove ___ with his last ounce of

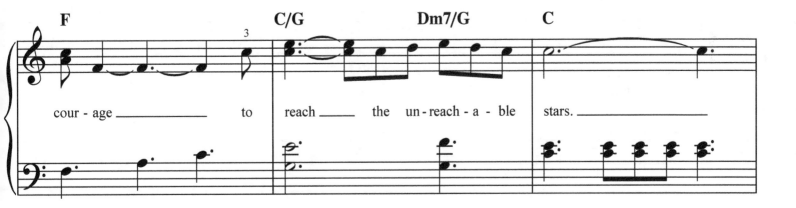

cour-age ___ to reach ___ the un-reach-a-ble stars. ___

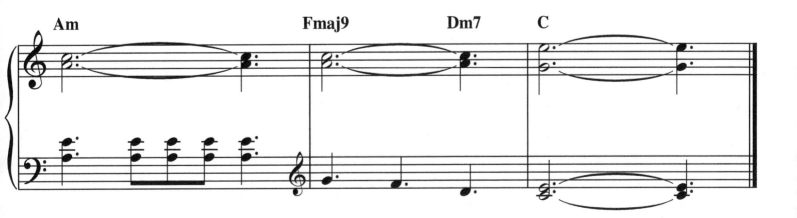

# JUST IN TIME
## from BELLS ARE RINGING

Words by BETTY COMDEN and ADOLPH GREEN
Music by JULE STYNE

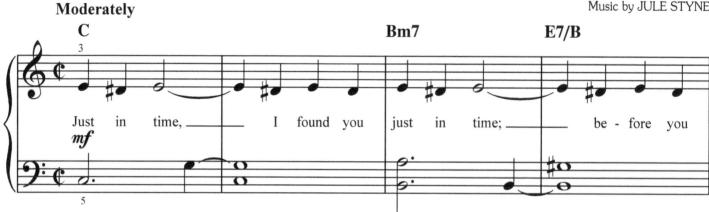

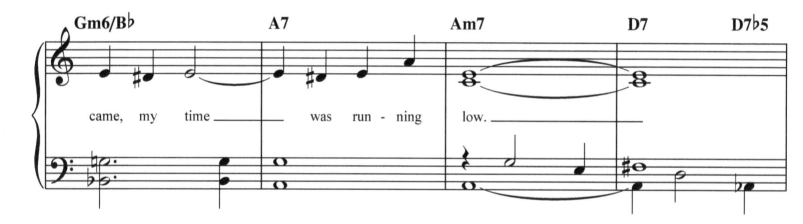

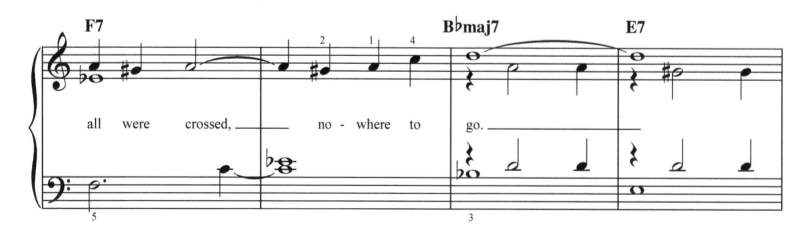

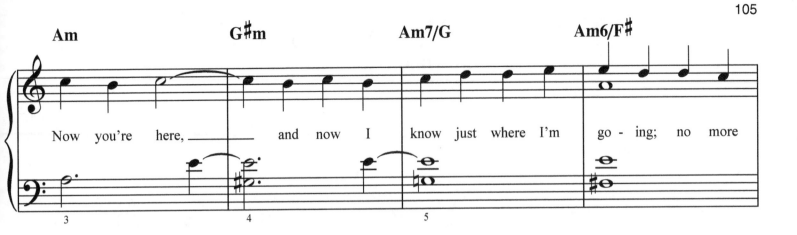

Now you're here, _____ and now I know just where I'm go-ing; no more

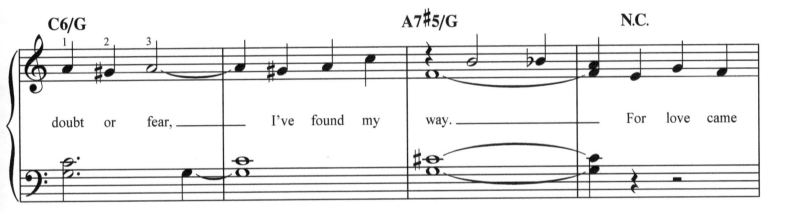

doubt or fear, _____ I've found my way. _____ For love came

just in time, _____ you found me just in time, _____ and changed my

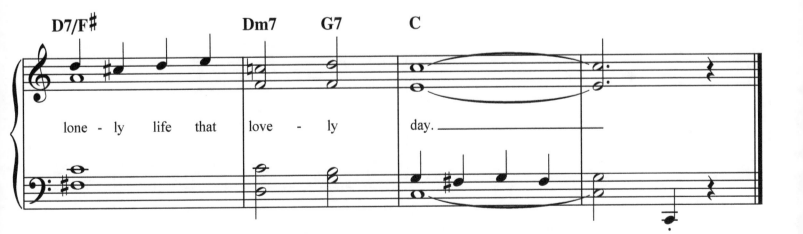

lone-ly life that love-ly day. _____

# THE LADY IS A TRAMP

## from BABES IN ARMS

Words by LORENZ HART
Music by RICHARD RODGERS

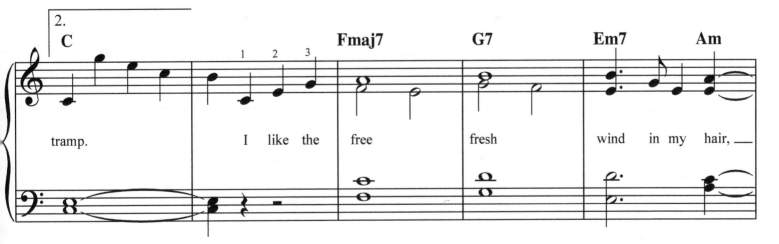

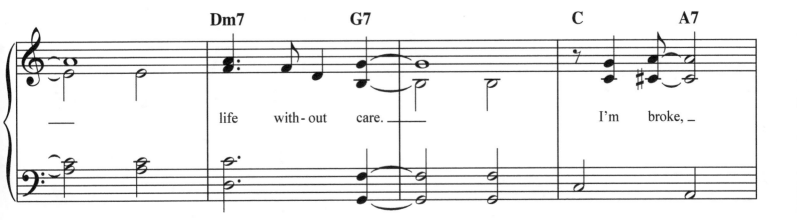

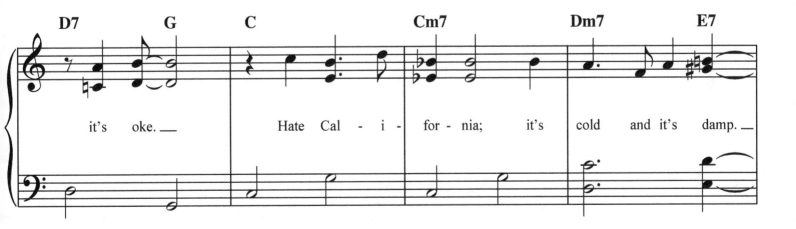

# LULLABY OF BROADWAY

**from 42nd Street**

Words by AL DUBIN
Music by HARRY WARREN

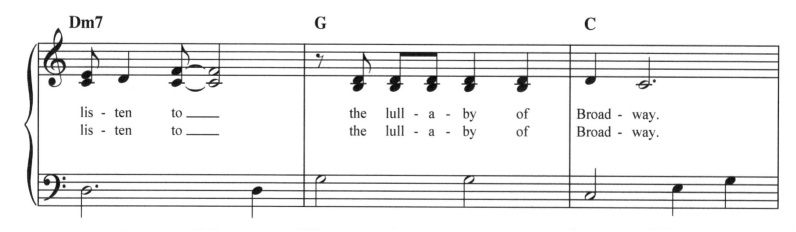

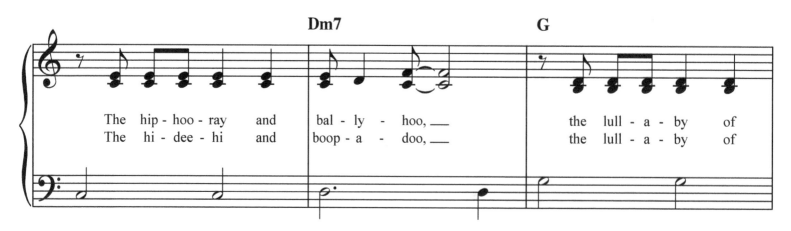

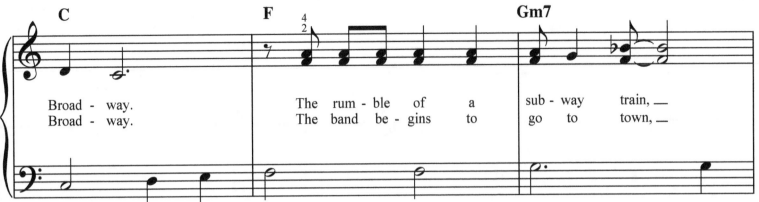

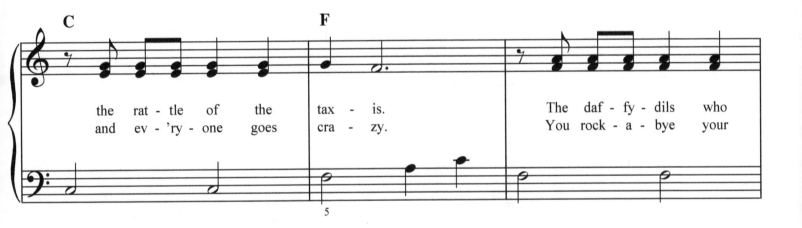

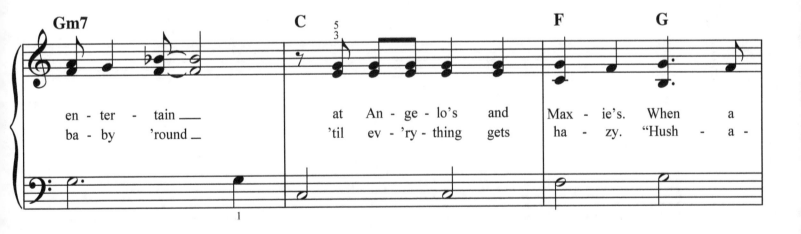

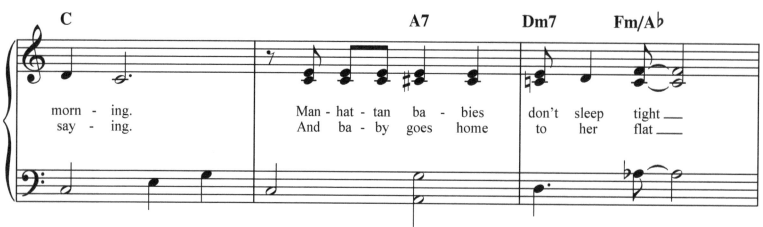

morn - ing.
say - ing.
Man - hat - tan ba - bies
And ba - by goes home
don't sleep tight ___
to her flat ___

un - til the
to sleep all
dawn:
day:
Good - night,

ba - by.
Good - night,

milk - man's on his way. ___
Sleep tight,

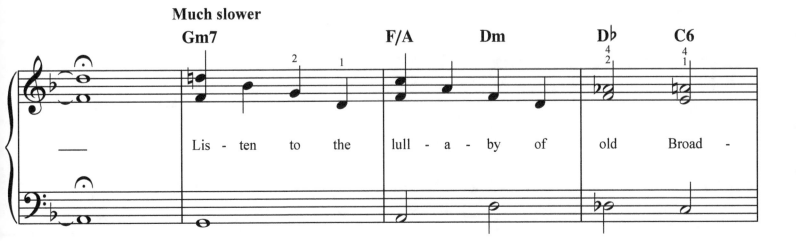

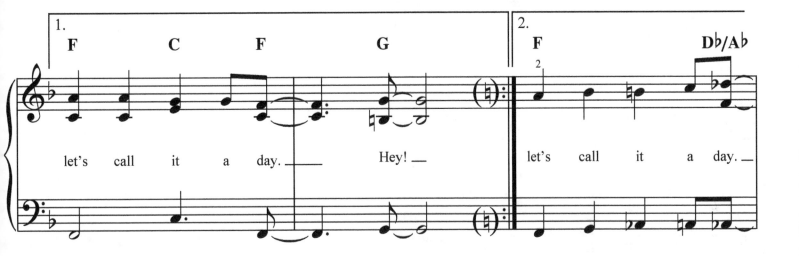

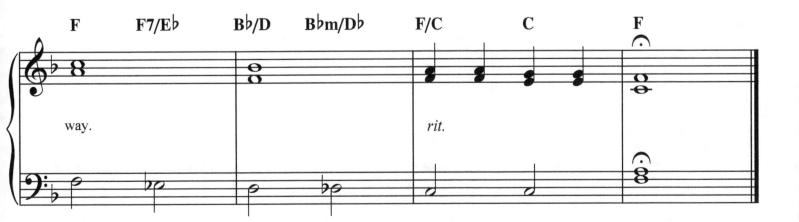

# MEMORY

### from CATS

Music by ANDREW LLOYD WEBBER
Text by TREVOR NUNN after T.S. ELIOT

**Moderately**

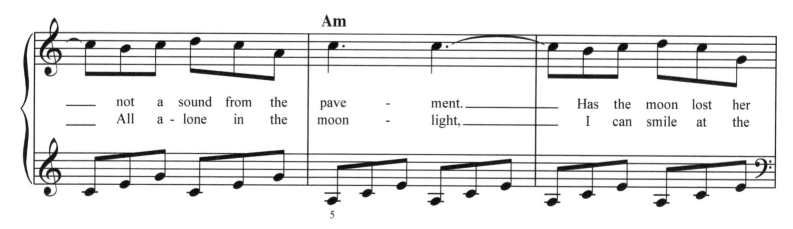

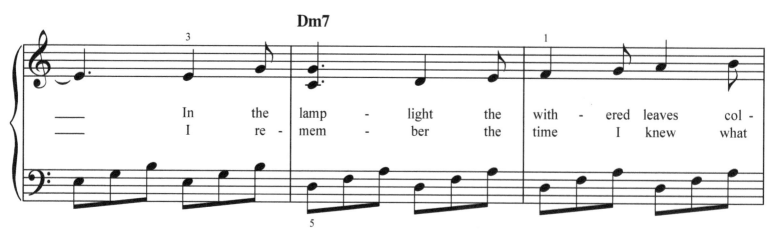

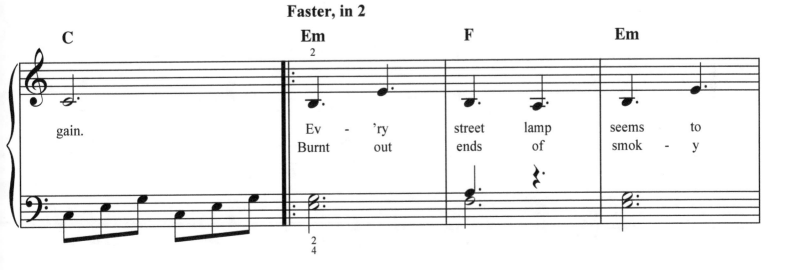

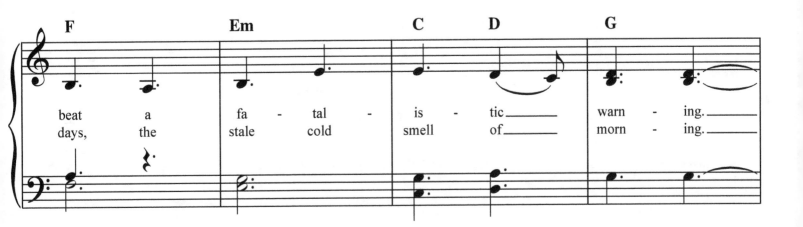

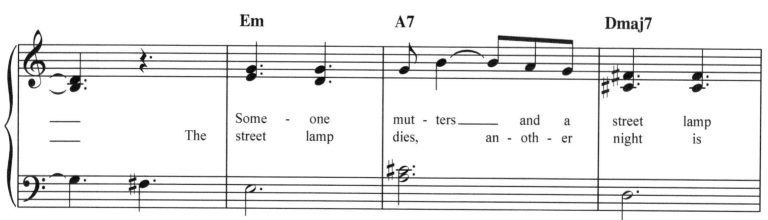

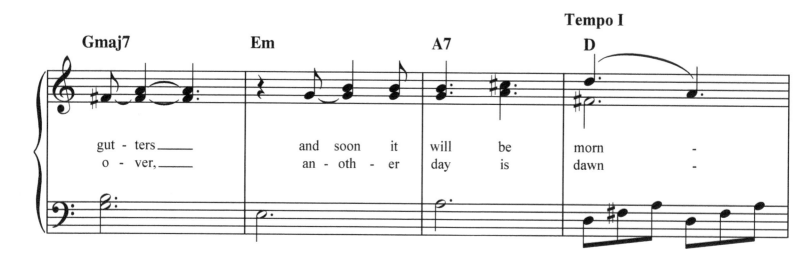

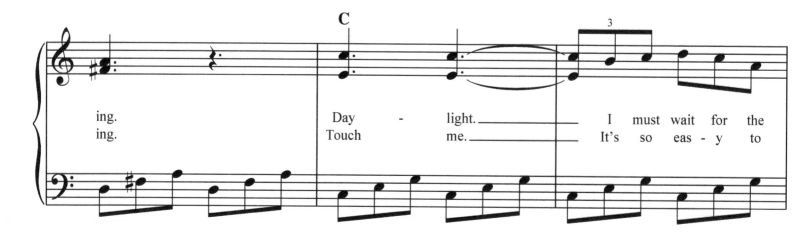

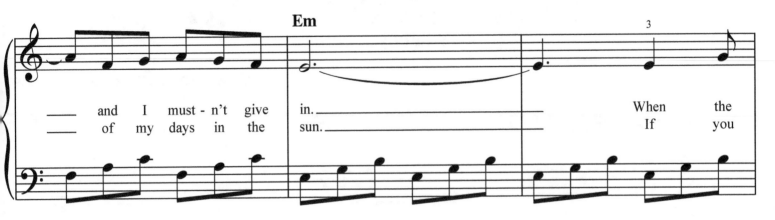

Em

and I must-n't give in. When the
of my days in the sun. If you

Dm7                                    Am

dawn comes to - night will be a mem - o - ry, too,
touch me, you'll un - der - stand a what hap - pi - ness is.

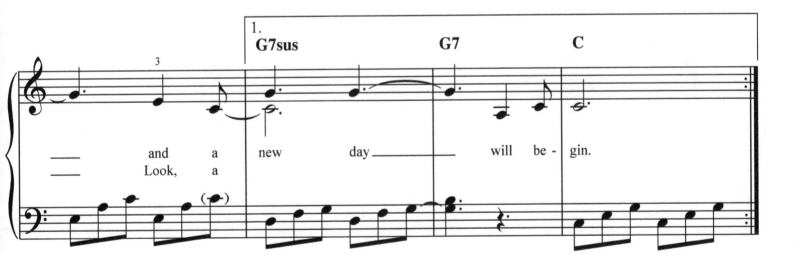

1.
G7sus                G7              C

and a new day will be - gin.
Look, a

2.
G7sus                G7              C

new day has be - gun.

# NEVER NEVER LAND

## from PETER PAN

Lyric by BETTY COMDEN and ADOLPH GREEN
Music by JULE STYNE

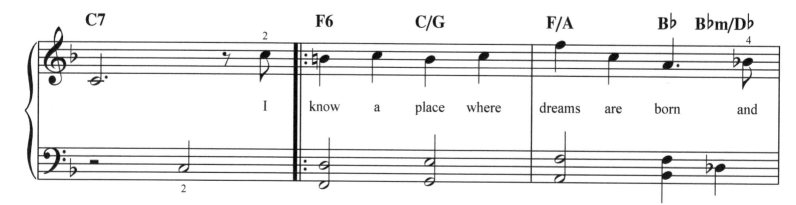

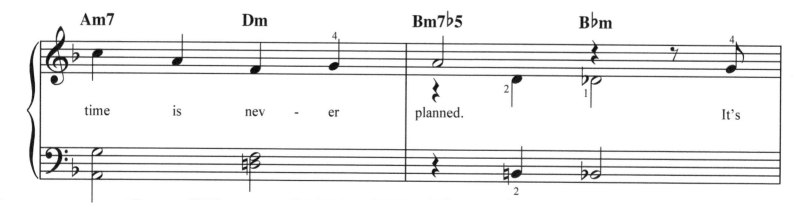

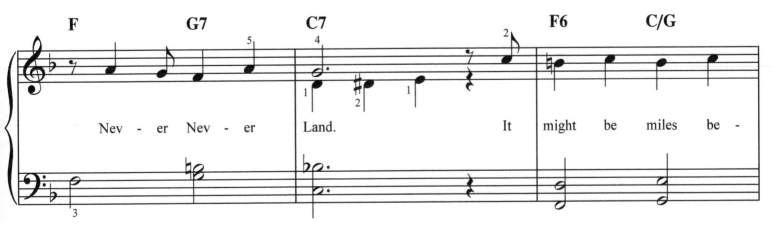

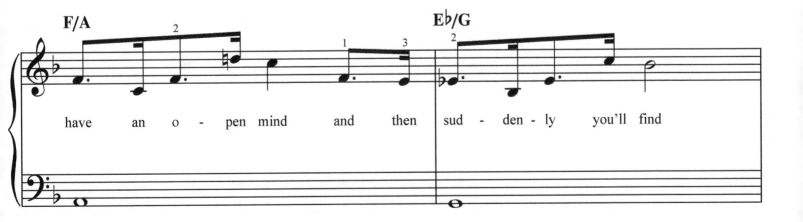

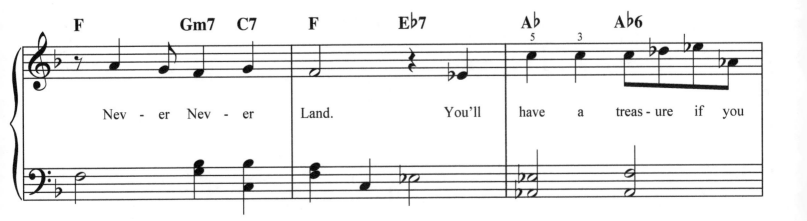

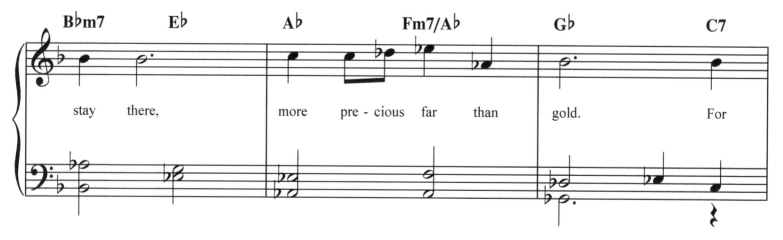

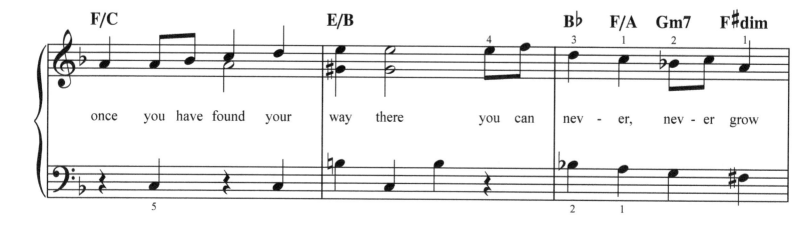

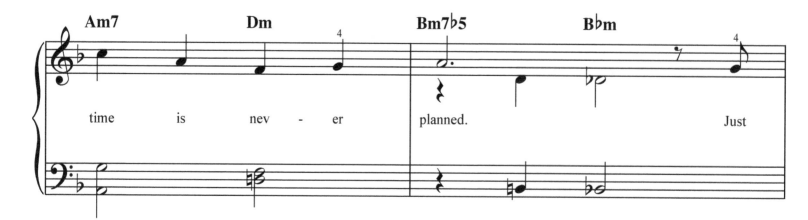

think of love - ly things and your heart will fly on wings, for -

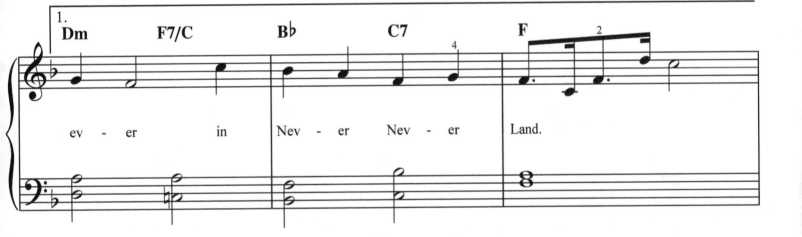

ev - er in Nev - er Nev - er Land.

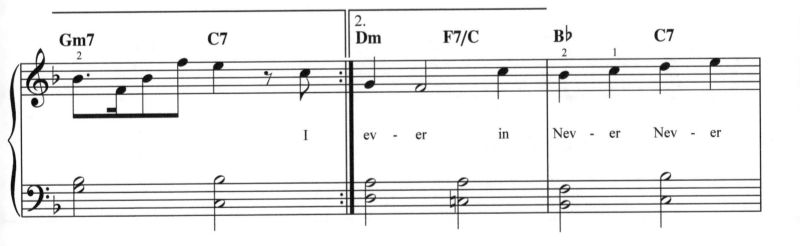

I ev - er in Nev - er Nev - er

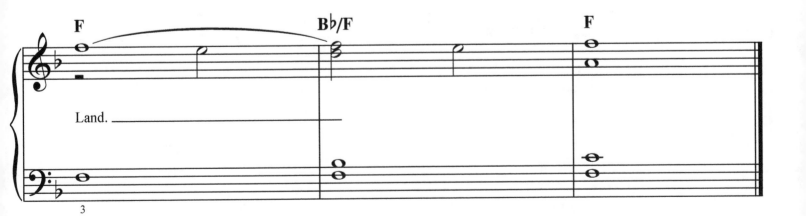

Land.

# OH, WHAT A BEAUTIFUL MORNIN'
## from OKLAHOMA!

Lyrics by OSCAR HAMMERSTEIN II
Music by RICHARD RODGERS

**Swaying**

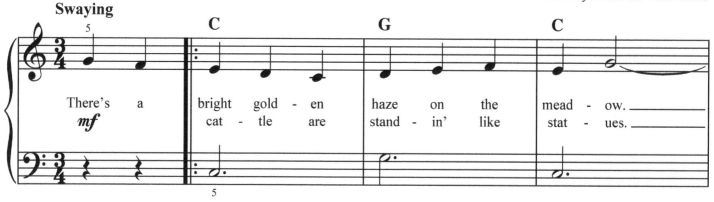

There's a bright gold - en haze on the mead - ow. _____
cat - tle are stand - in' like stat - ues.

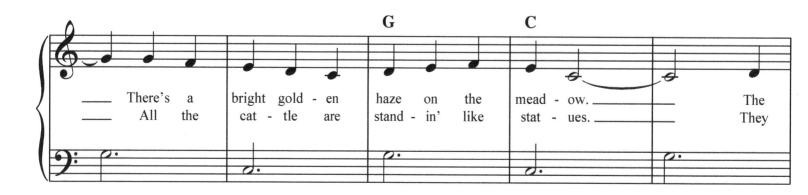

_____ There's a bright gold - en haze on the mead - ow. _____ The
_____ All the cat - tle are stand - in' like stat - ues. _____ They

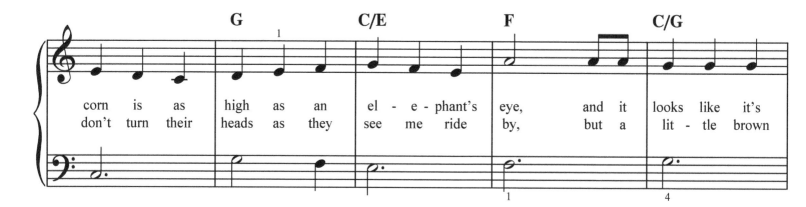

corn is as high as an el - e - phant's eye, and it looks like it's
don't turn their heads as they see me ride by, but a lit - tle brown

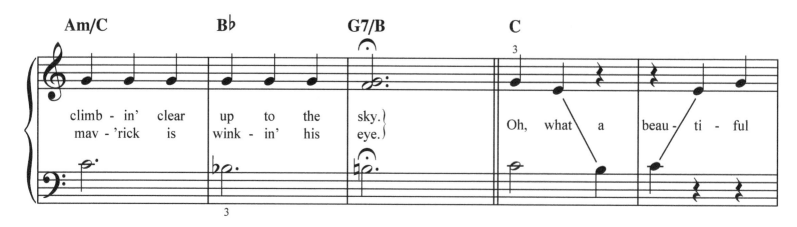

climb - in' clear up to the sky.)
mav - 'rick is wink - in' his eye.)
Oh, what a beau - ti - ful

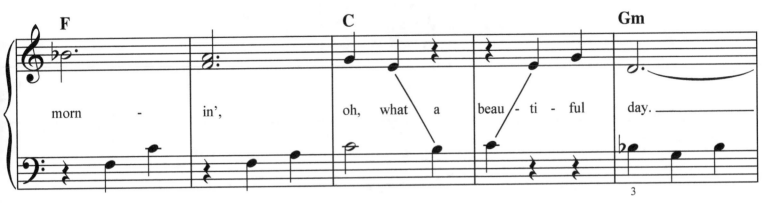

morn - in', oh, what a beau - ti - ful day. _____

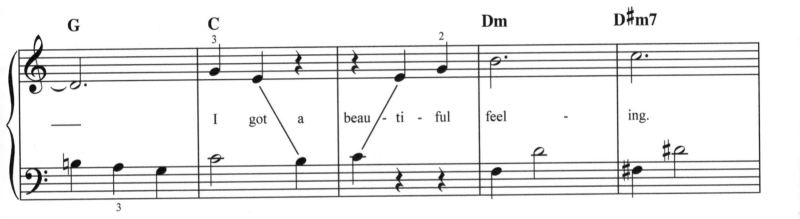

_____ I got a beau - ti - ful feel - ing.

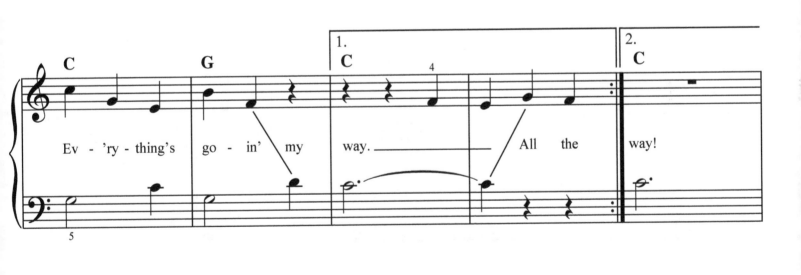

Ev - 'ry - thing's go - in' my way. _____ All the way!

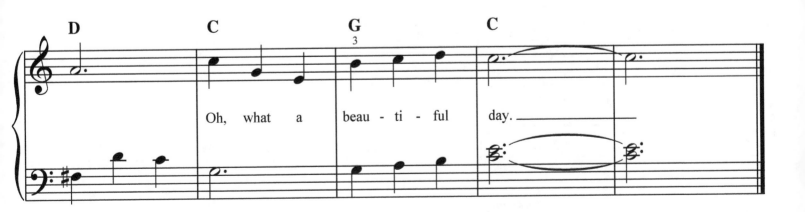

Oh, what a beau - ti - ful day. _____

# OL' MAN RIVER

**from SHOW BOAT**

Lyrics by OSCAR HAMMERSTEIN II
Music by JEROME KERN

**Slowly, in 2**

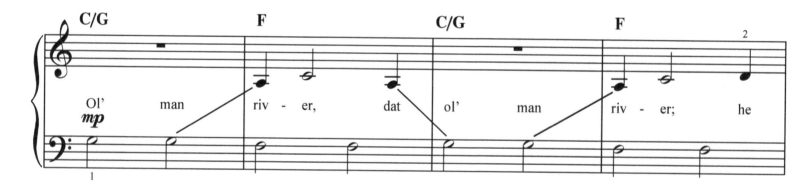

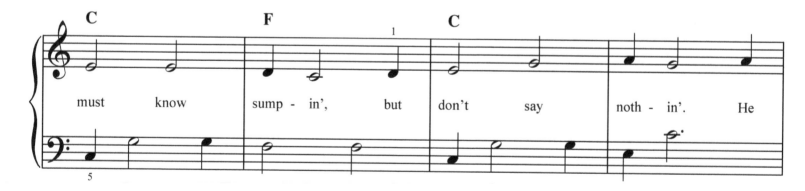

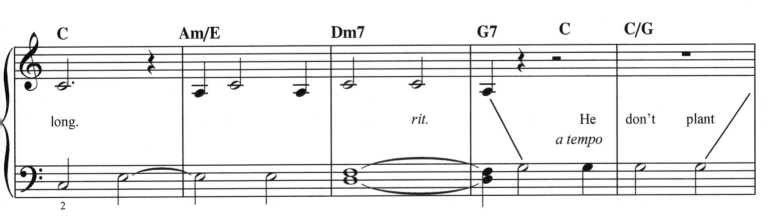

long.

*rit.*  *a tempo*  He don't plant

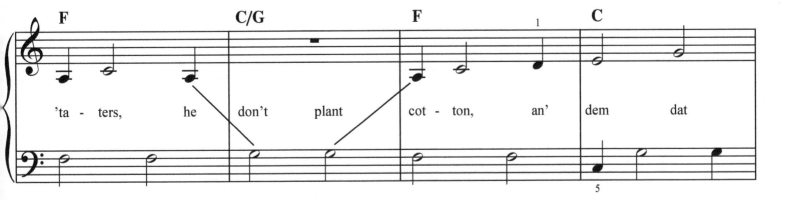

'ta - ters, he don't plant cot - ton, an' dem dat

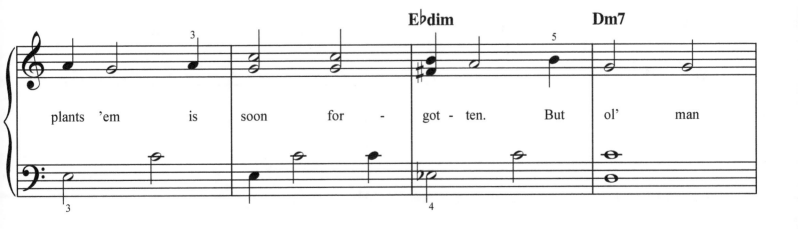

plants 'em is soon for - got - ten. But ol' man

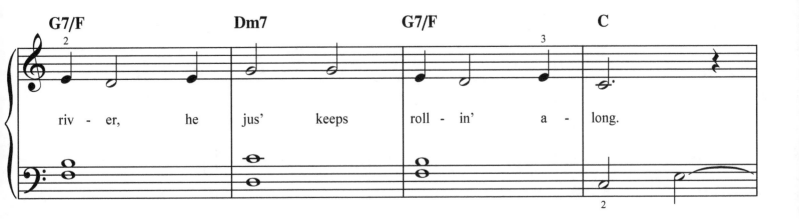

riv - er, he jus' keeps roll - in' a - long.

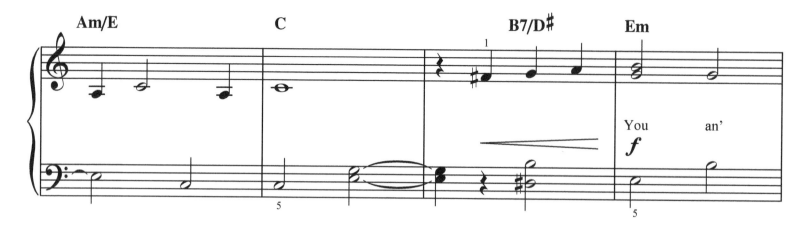

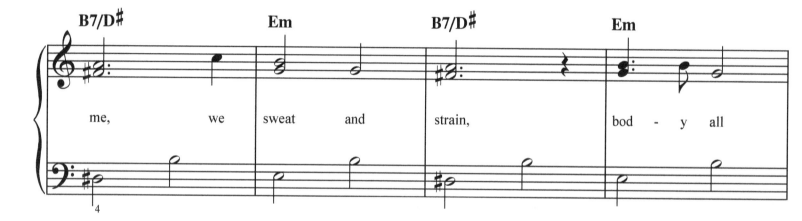

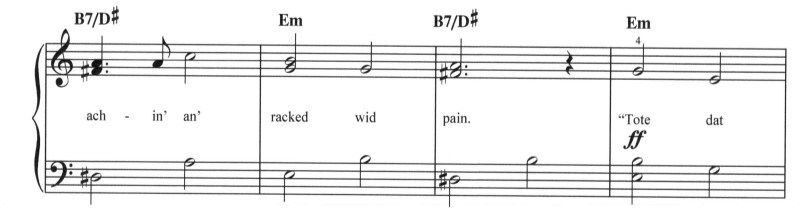

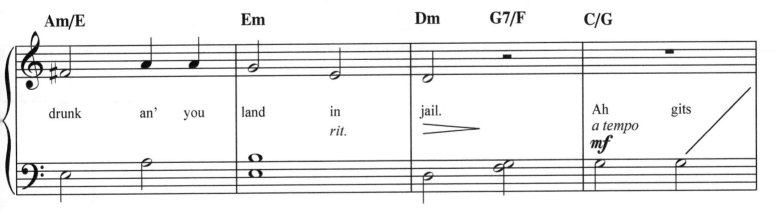

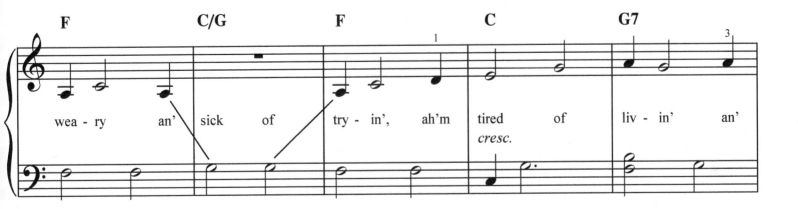

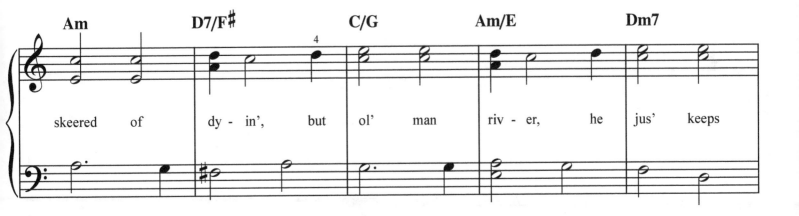

# ON A CLEAR DAY

## (You Can See Forever)

### from ON A CLEAR DAY YOU CAN SEE FOREVER

Words by ALAN JAY LERNER
Music by BURTON LANE

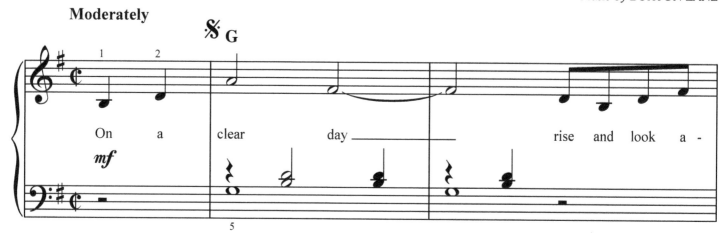

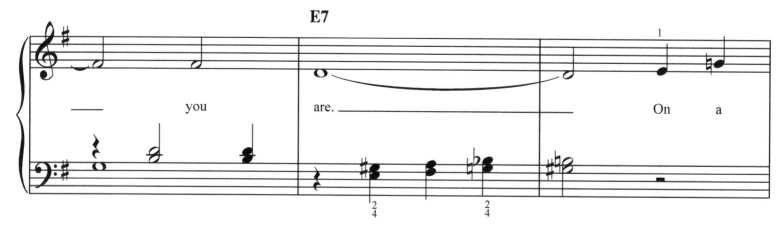

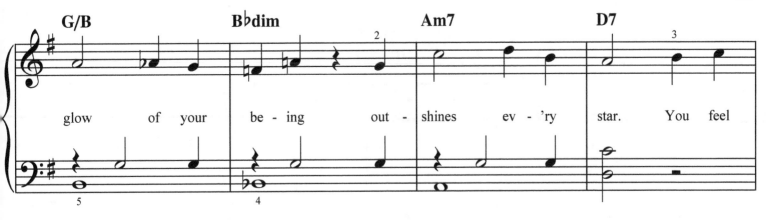

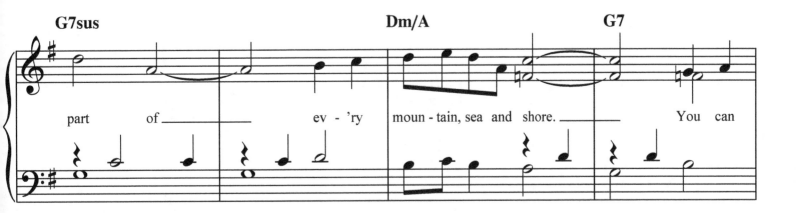

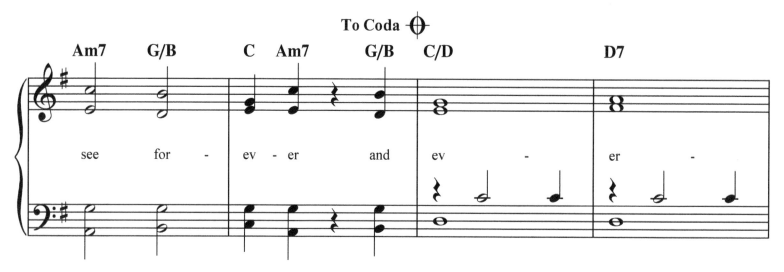

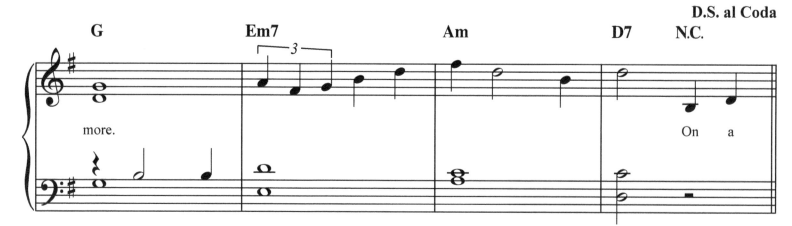

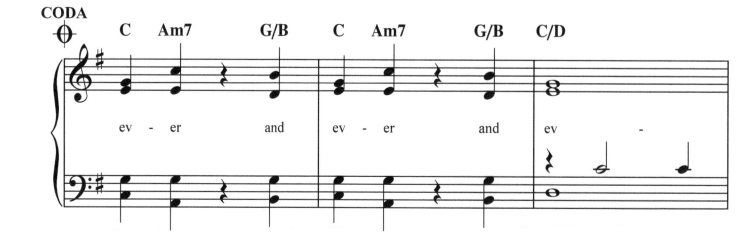

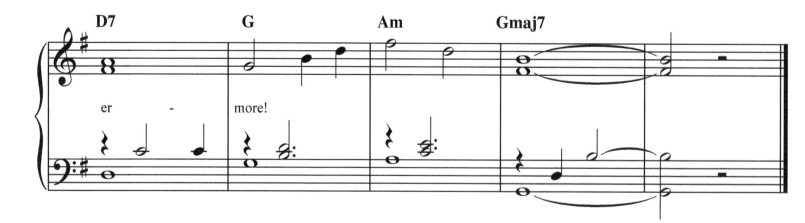

# ONCE IN LOVE WITH AMY

## from WHERE'S CHARLEY?

By FRANK LOESSER

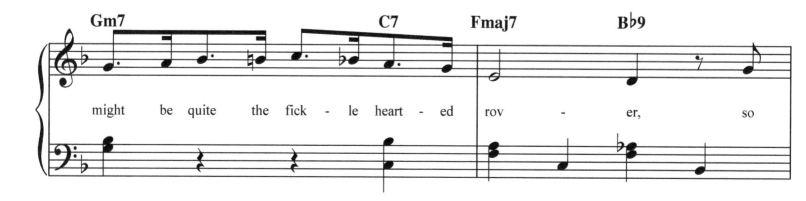

might be quite the fick - le heart - ed rov - er, so

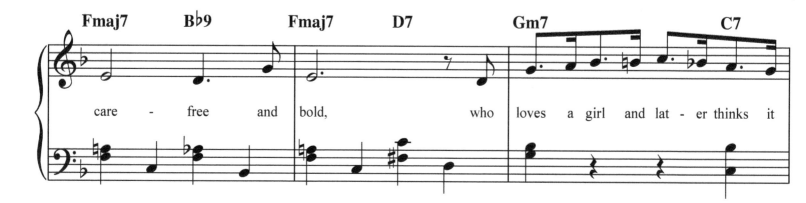

care - free and bold, who loves a girl and lat - er thinks it

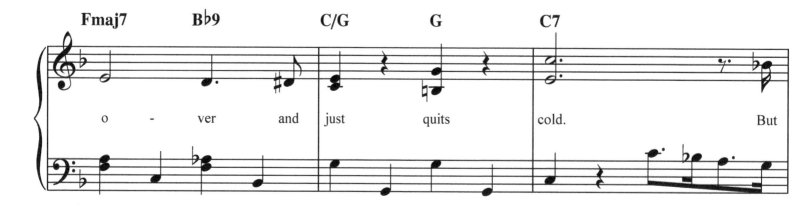

o - ver and just quits cold. But

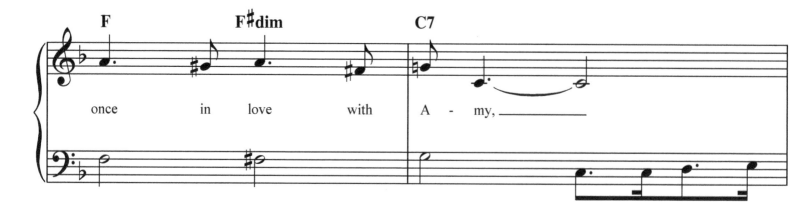

once in love with A - my, _____

F | F#dim | C7 | F | F7/E♭

al - ways in love with A - my. _____ Ev - er and ev - er

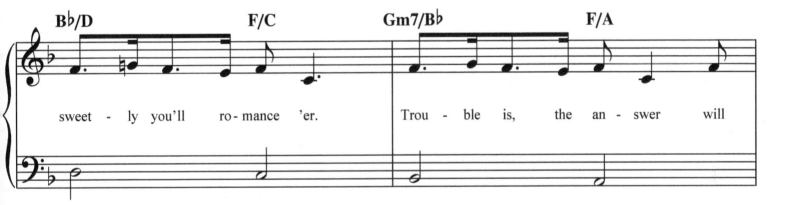

B♭/D | F/C | Gm7/B♭ | F/A

sweet - ly you'll ro - mance 'er. Trou - ble is, the an - swer will

A7/C# | D7 | Gm

be that A - my'd rath - er stay in

G7 | C7/E | F

love with me.

# POPULAR
## from the Broadway Musical WICKED

Music and Lyrics by
STEPHEN SCHWARTZ

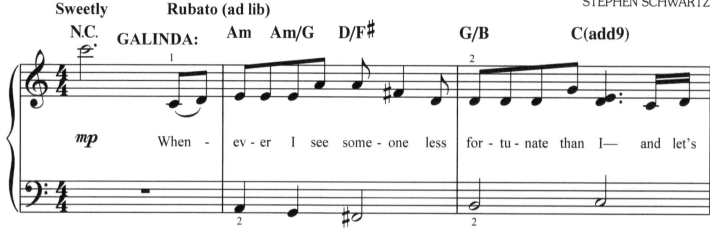

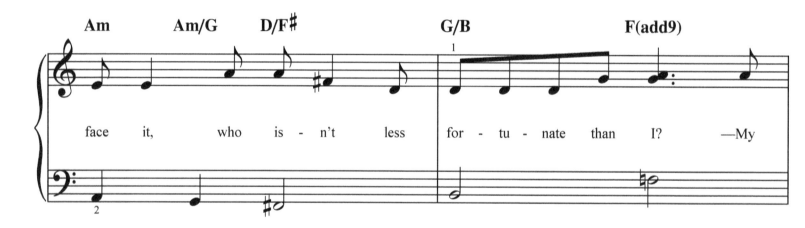

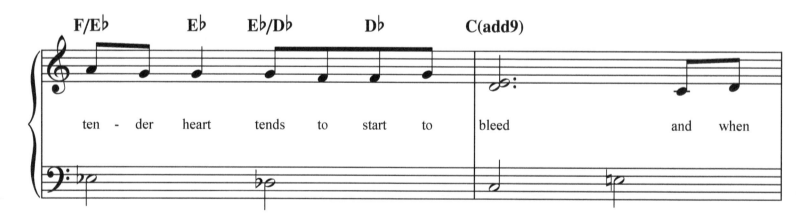

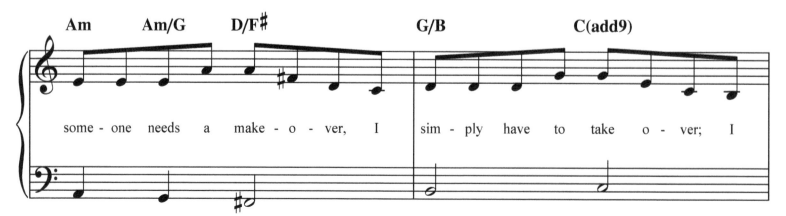

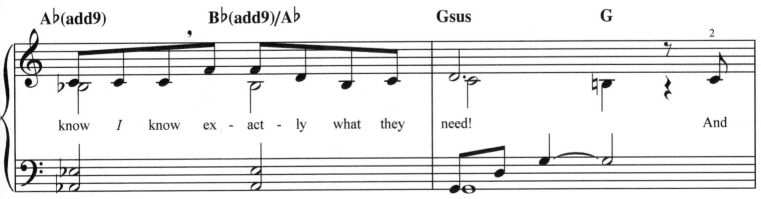

know *I* know ex - act - ly what they need! And

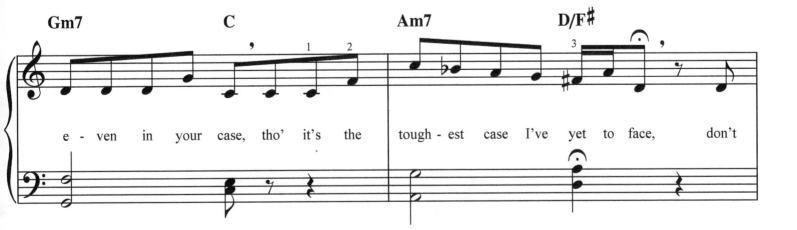

e - ven in your case, tho' it's the tough - est case I've yet to face, don't

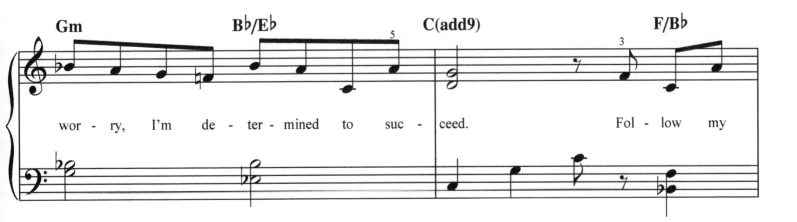

wor - ry, I'm de - ter - mined to suc - ceed. Fol - low my

lead and yes, in - deed you will be...

*rit.*

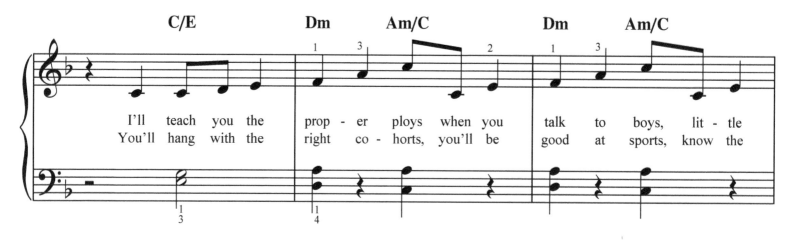

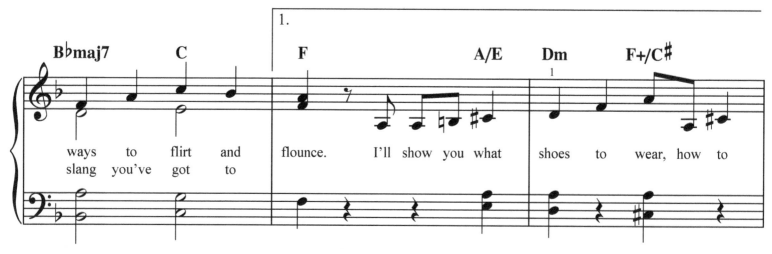

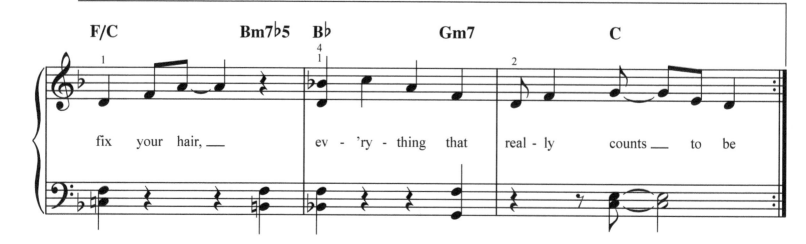

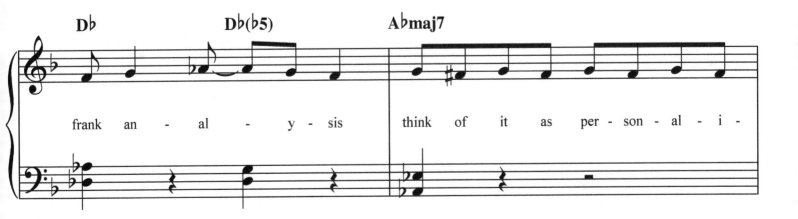

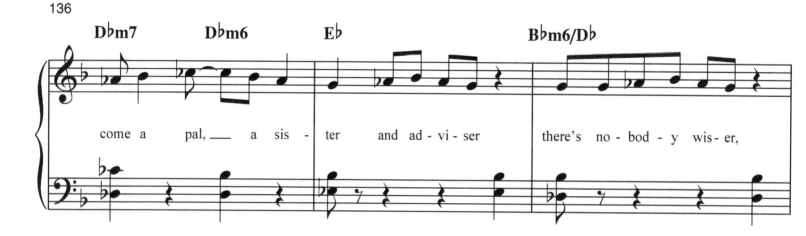

come a pal,__ a sis - ter and ad - vi - ser there's no - bod - y wis - er,

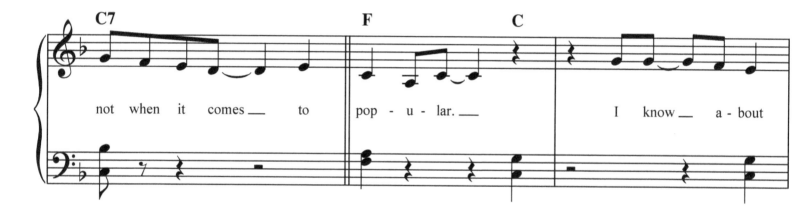

not when it comes __ to pop - u - lar. __ I know __ a - bout

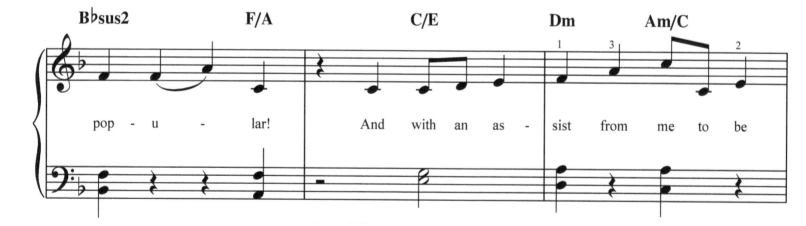

pop - u - lar! And with an as - sist from me to be

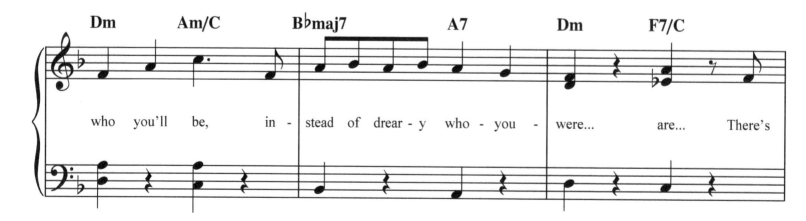

who you'll be, in - stead of drear - y who - you - were... are... There's

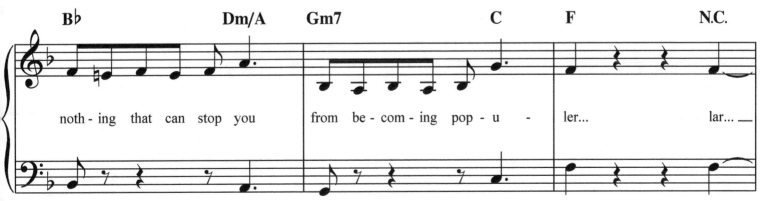

noth - ing that can stop you from be - com - ing pop - u - ler... lar...

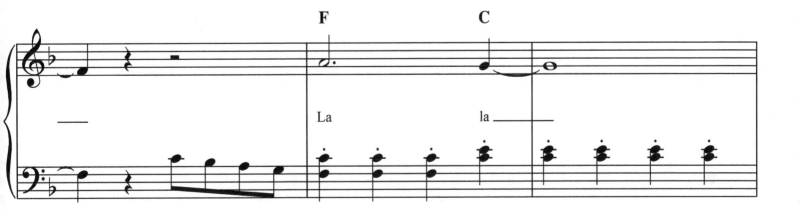

La la la

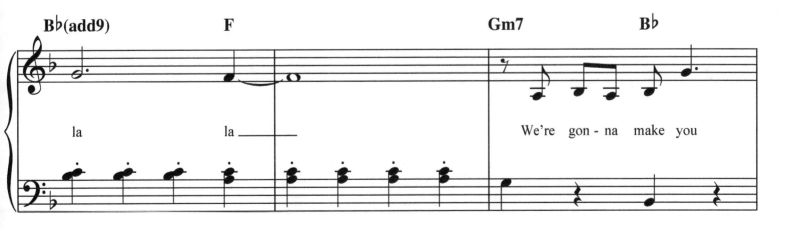

la la We're gon - na make you

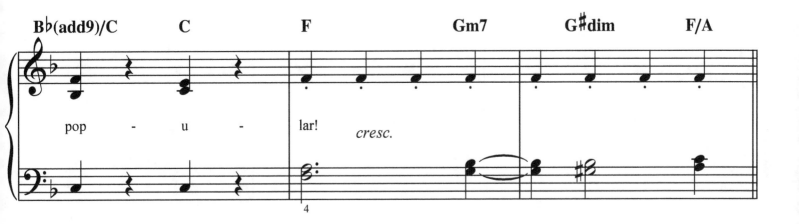

pop - u - lar! *cresc.*

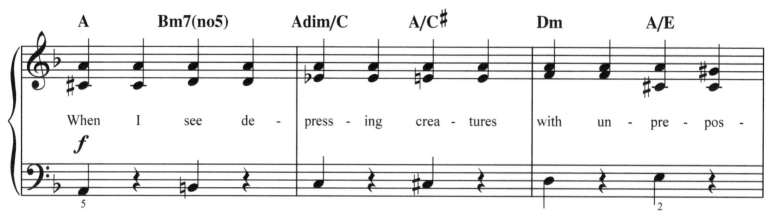

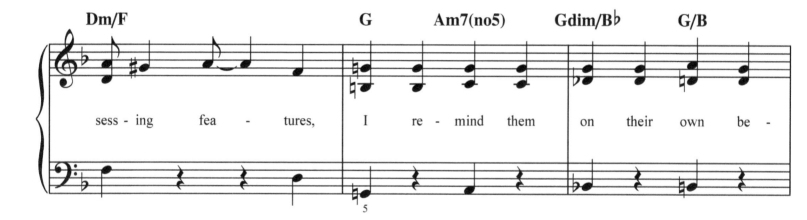

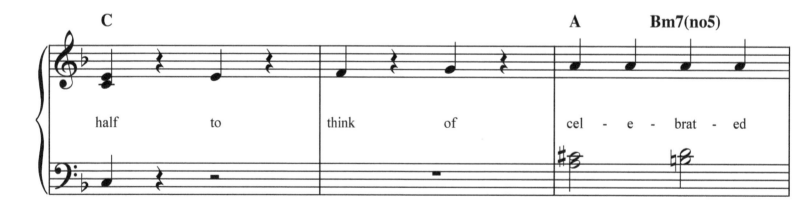

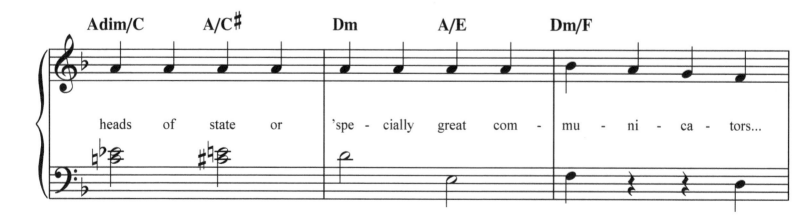

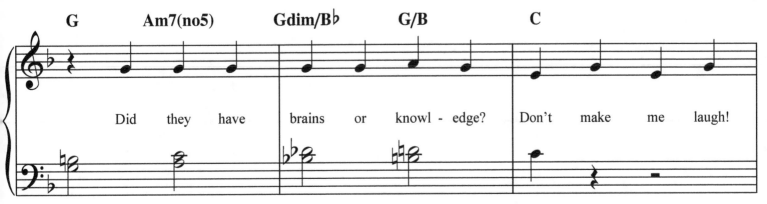

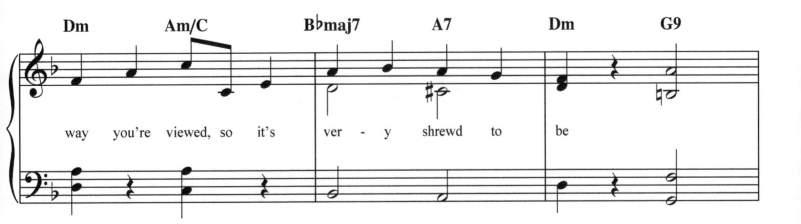

**Gm7** **B♭** **C** **F**

ver - y, ver - y pop - u - lar like me!

*dim.*

**Freely**
**Dm** **Am/C** **Dm** **Am/C**

*rit.* And tho' you pro - test __ your dis - in - ter - est, __

*mp*

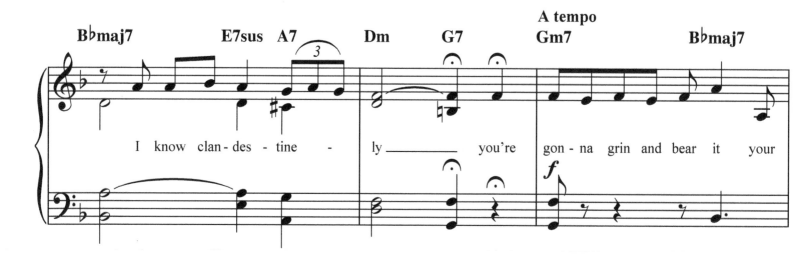

**B♭maj7** **E7sus** **A7** **Dm** **G7** **A tempo** **Gm7** **B♭maj7**

I know clan - des - tine - ly __ you're gon - na grin and bear it your

*f*

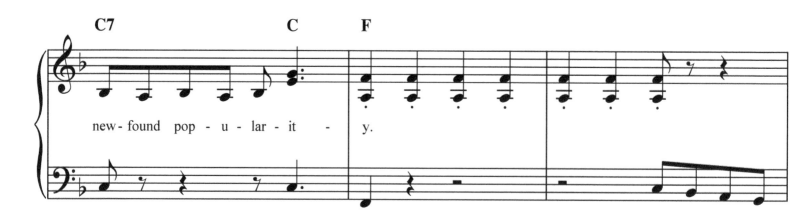

**C7** **C** **F**

new - found pop - u - lar - it - y.

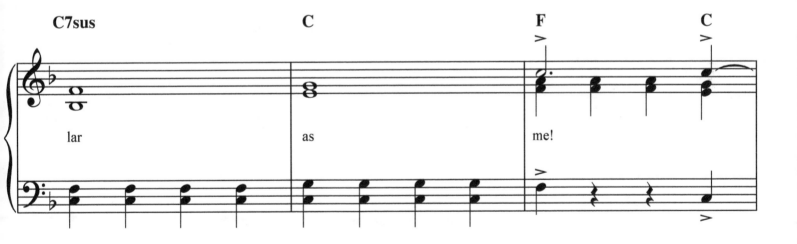

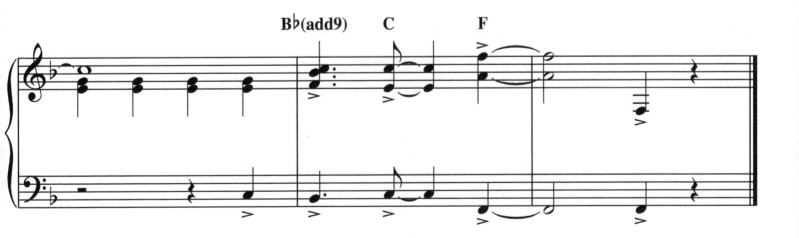

# SEVENTY SIX TROMBONES

**from Meredith Willson's THE MUSIC MAN**

By MEREDITH WILLSON

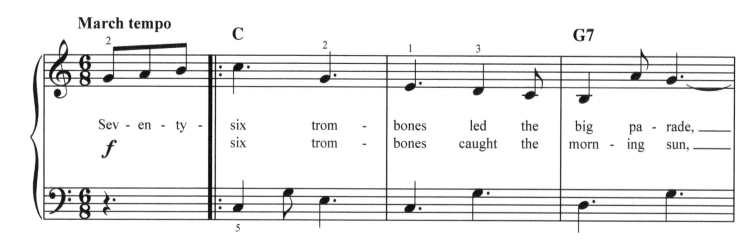

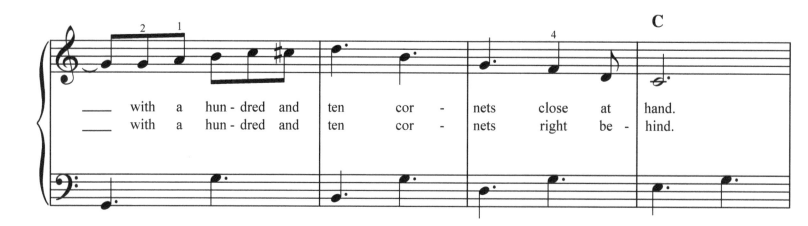

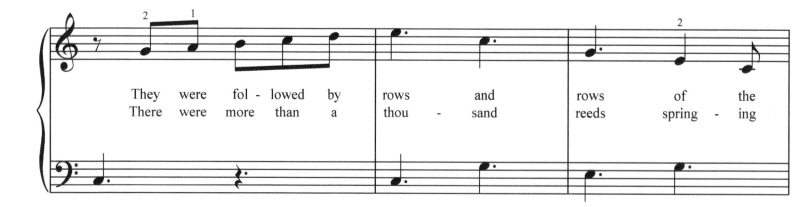

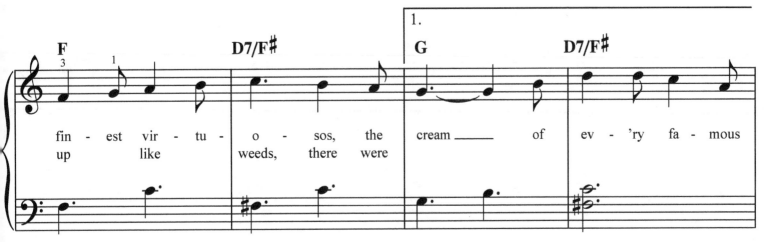

fin - est vir - tu - o - sos, the cream _____ of ev - 'ry fa - mous
up like weeds, there were

band. Sev - en - ty - horns _____ of ev - 'ry shape and

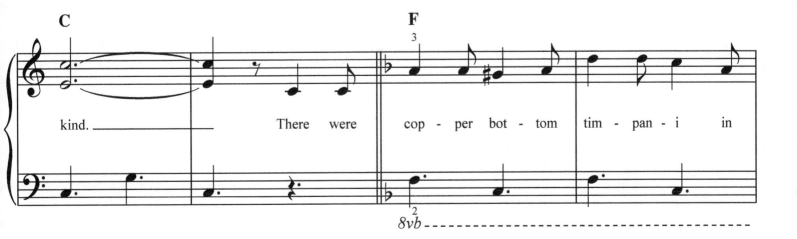

kind. _____ There were cop - per bot - tom tim - pan - i in

horse pla - toons _____ thun - der - ing, thun - der - ing,

all a - long the way. Dou - ble bell eu - pho - ni - ums and

*(8vb)*

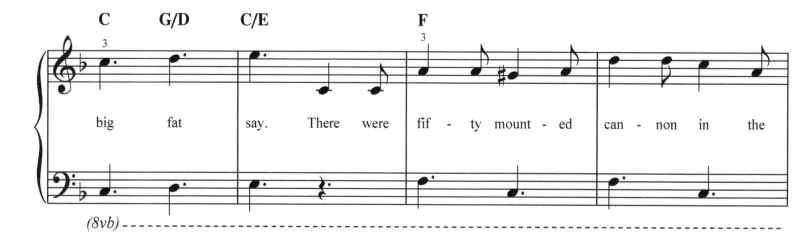

big bas - soons, each bas - soon hav - ing his

*(8vb)*

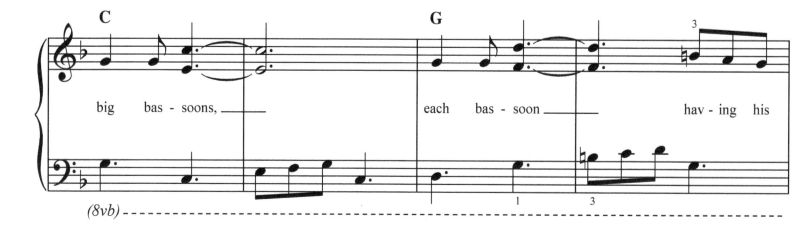

big fat say. There were fif - ty mount - ed can - non in the

*(8vb)*

bat - ter - y, thun - der - ing, thun - der - ing,

*(8vb)*

F · C · F · | loud - er than be - fore. | Clar - i - nets of ev - 'ry size and

C7/G · E7 · Am · Gm · C7 | trum - pet - ers who'd im - pro - vise a full oc - tave high - er than the

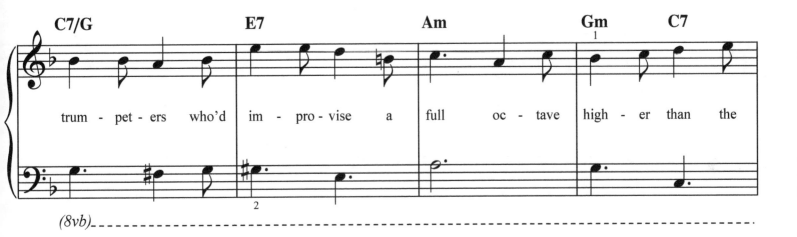

F · G · C | score. | Sev - en - ty - six trom -

G7 | bones led the big pa - rade ___ when the or - der to march rang

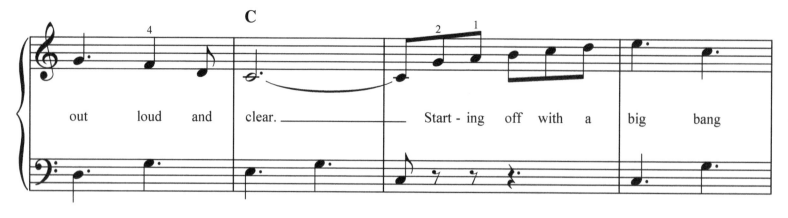

out loud and clear._____ Start - ing off with a big bang

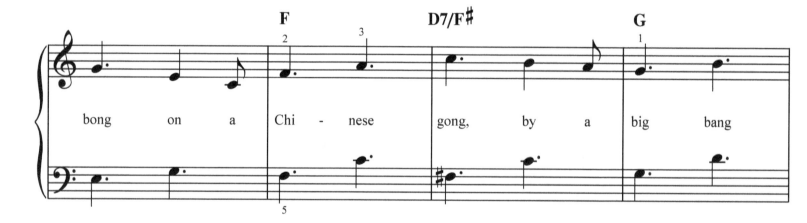

bong on a Chi - nese gong, by a big bang

bong - er at the rear. Sev - en - ty - six trom -

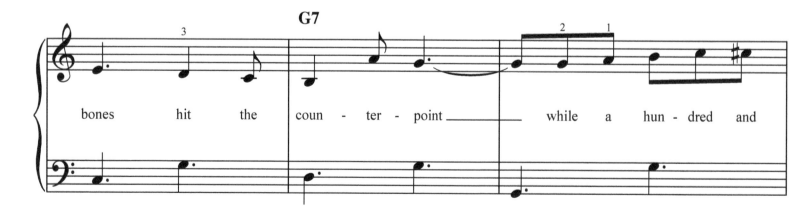

bones hit the coun - ter - point_____ while a hun - dred and

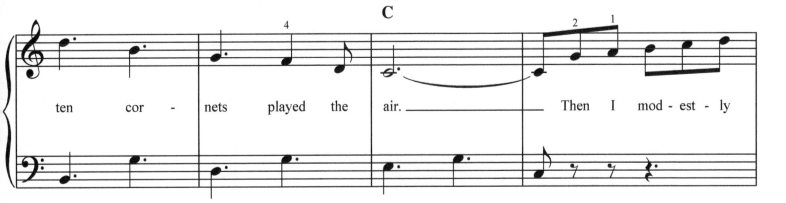

ten cor - nets played the air. _____ Then I mod - est - ly

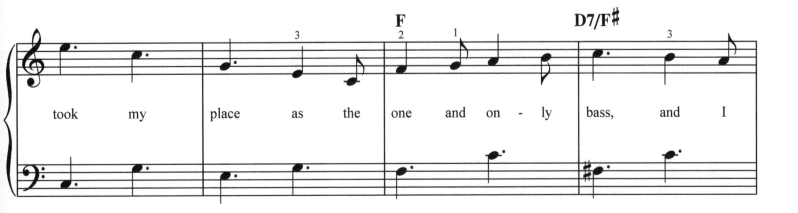

took my place as the one and on - ly bass, and I

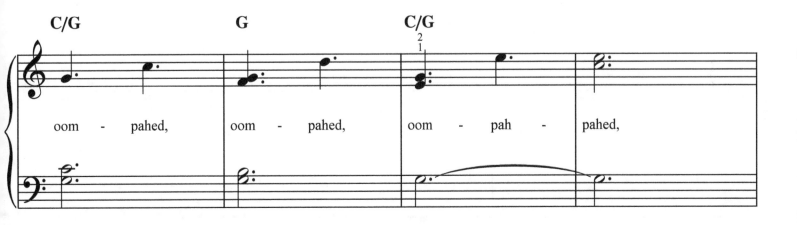

oom - pahed, oom - pahed, oom - pah - pahed,

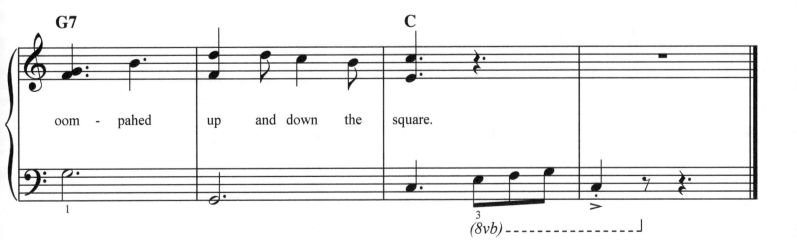

oom - pahed up and down the square.

(8vb) _ _ _ _ _ _ _ _ _ _ _ _ _ _ _ ⌐

# SHE LOVES ME

### from SHE LOVES ME

Words by SHELDON HARNICK
Music by JERRY BOCK

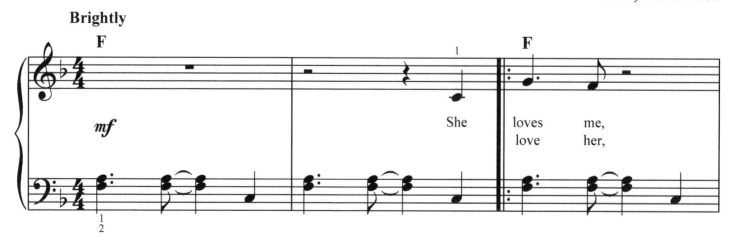

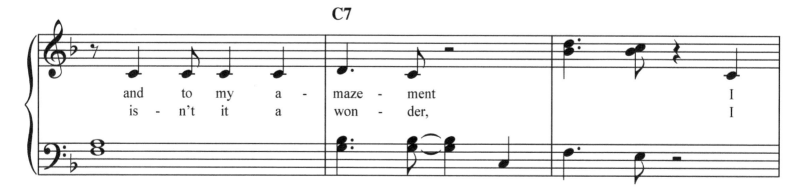

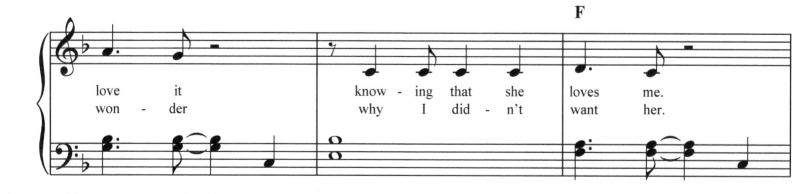

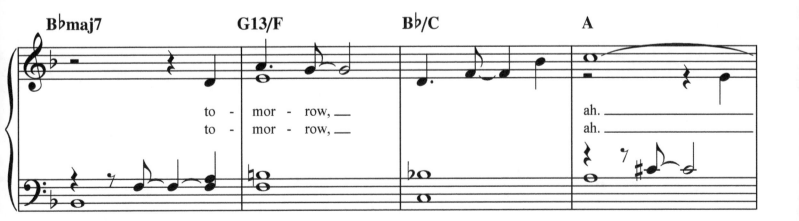

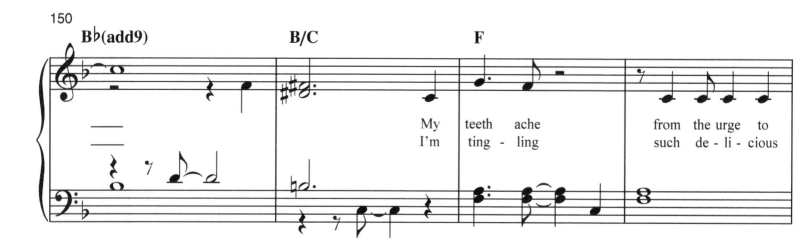

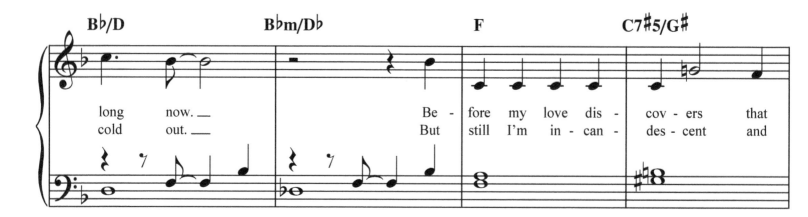

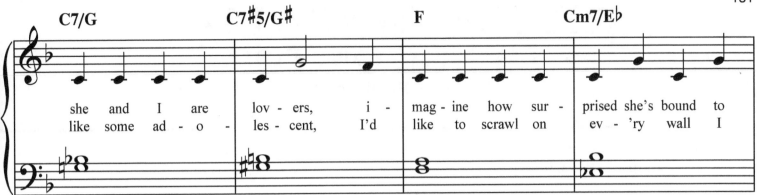

she   and   I   are
like   some   ad - o -

lov - ers,   i -
les - cent,   I'd

mag - ine   how   sur -
like   to   scrawl   on

prised   she's   bound   to
ev - 'ry   wall   I

be.
see.

She   loves   me, _____
She   loves   me, _____

1.

she
she

loves
loves

me.

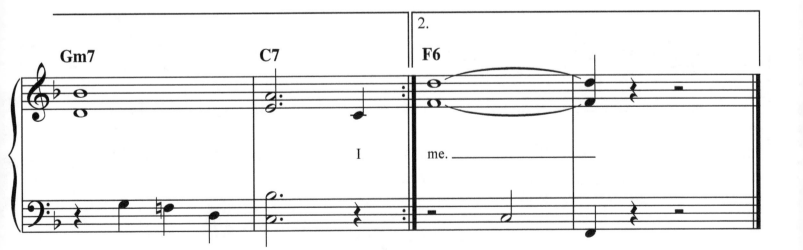

2.

I

me. _____

# THE SURREY WITH THE FRINGE ON TOP

**from OKLAHOMA!**

Lyrics by OSCAR HAMMERSTEIN II
Music by RICHARD RODGERS

**Easily, with a bounce**

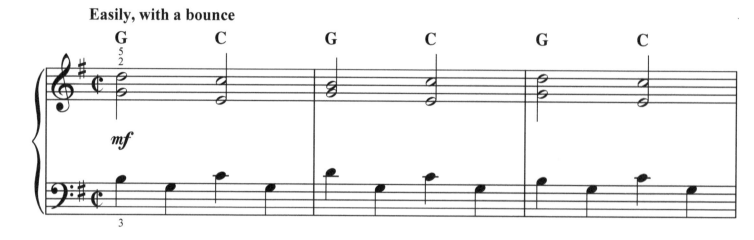

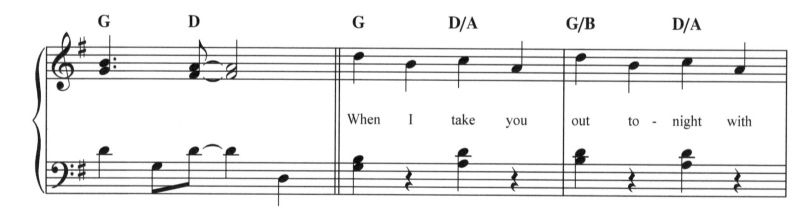

When I take you out to-night with

me, _____ Hon - ey, here's the

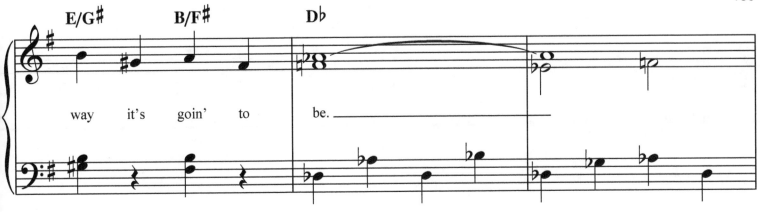

E/G# B/F# Db

way it's goin' to be. ___

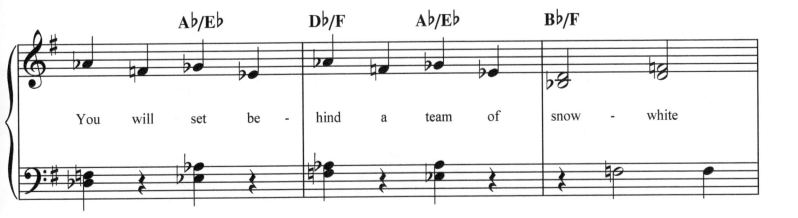

Ab/Eb Db/F Ab/Eb Bb/F

You will set be - hind a team of snow - white

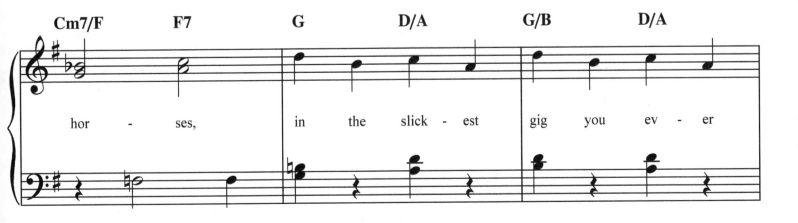

Cm7/F F7 G D/A G/B D/A

hor - ses, in the slick - est gig you ev - er

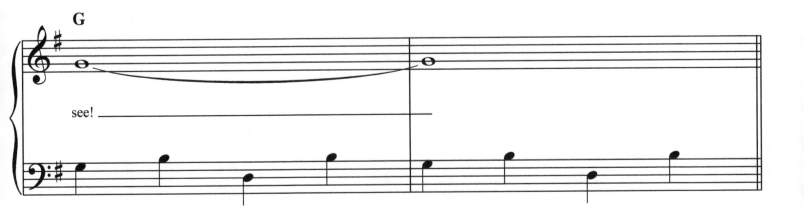

G

see! ___

153

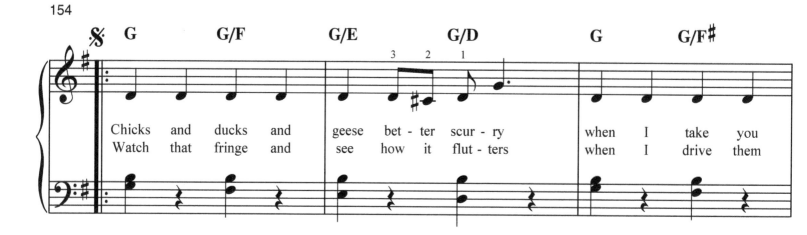

Chicks and ducks and geese bet-ter scur-ry when I take you
Watch that fringe and see how it flut-ters when I drive them

out in the sur-rey, when I take you out in the sur-rey with the
high step-pin' strut-ters, nos-ey pokes-'ll peek thru their shut-ters and their

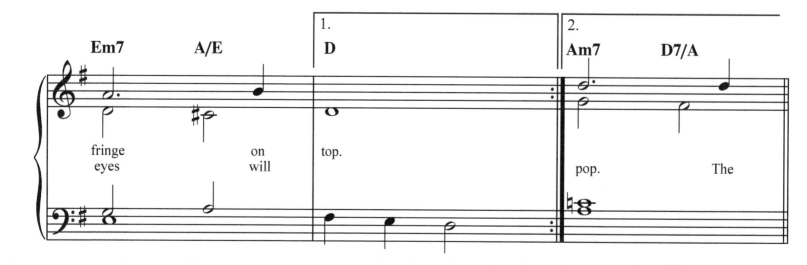

1.
fringe on top.
eyes will

2.
pop. The

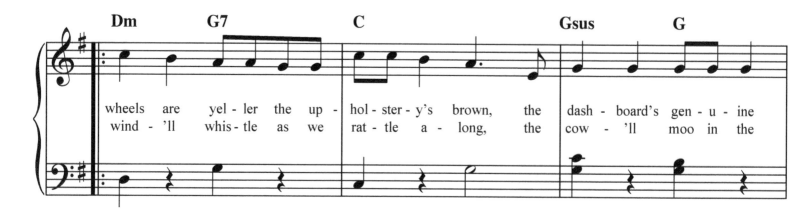

wheels are yel-ler the up-hol-ster-y's brown, the dash-board's gen-u-ine
wind-'ll whis-tle as we rat-tle a-long, the cow-'ll moo in the

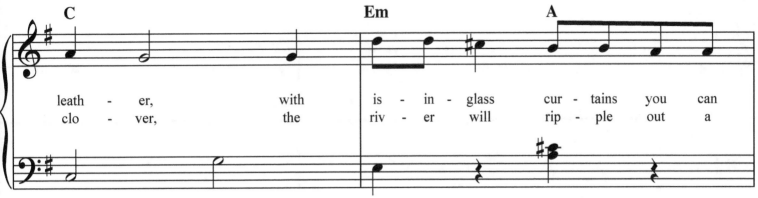

leath - er,
clo - ver,
with
the
is - in - glass cur - tains you can
riv - er will rip - ple out a

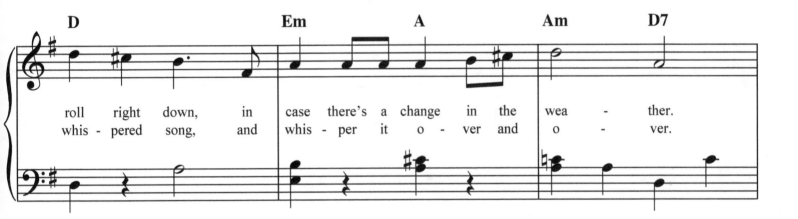

roll right down, in
whis - pered song, and
case there's a change in the
whis - per it o - ver and
wea - ther.
o - ver.

Two bright side - light's
Don't you wish y'd
wink - in' and blink - in'
go on for - ev - er,
ain't no fin - er
don't you wish y'd

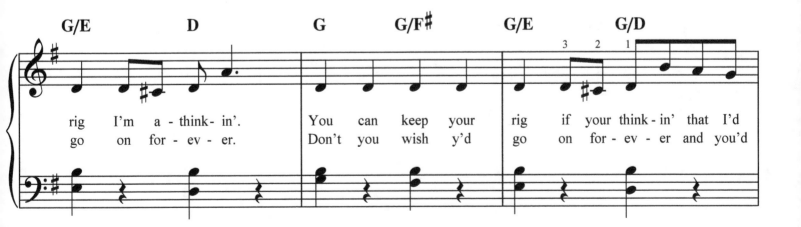

rig I'm a - think - in'.
go on for - ev - er.
You can keep your
Don't you wish y'd
rig if your think - in' that I'd
go on for - ev - er and you'd

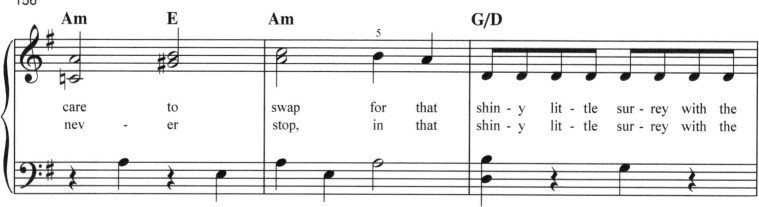

care        to          swap        for  that       shin - y   lit - tle  sur - rey  with  the
nev -    er        stop,        in   that       shin - y   lit - tle  sur - rey  with  the

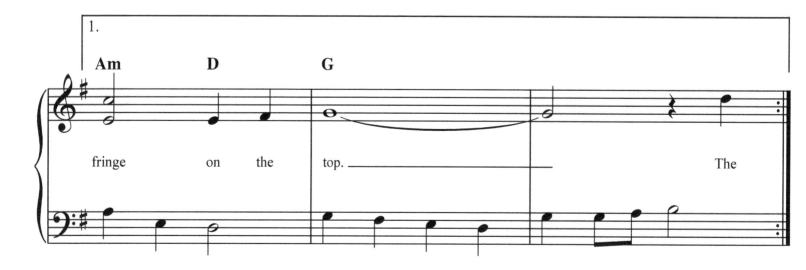

fringe        on    the       top. _____                              The

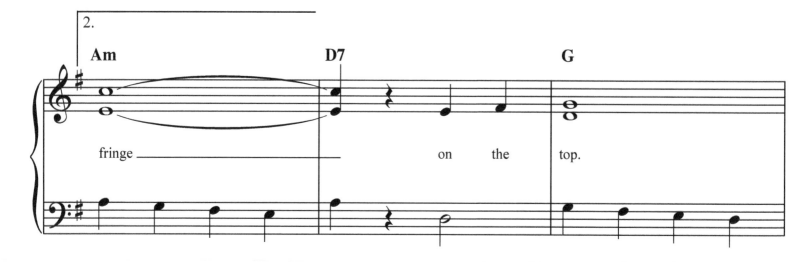

fringe _____                              on    the   top.

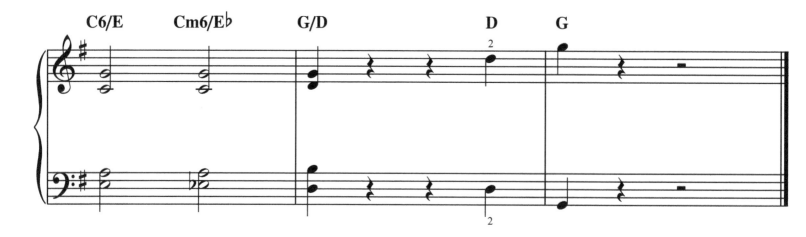

# SUNRISE, SUNSET
### from the Musical FIDDLER ON THE ROOF

Words by SHELDON HARNICK
Music by JERRY BOCK

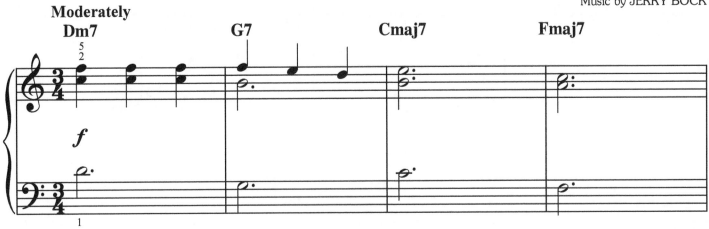

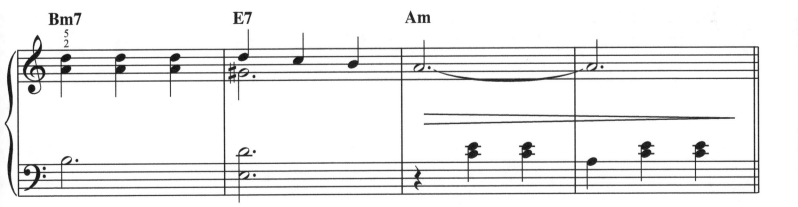

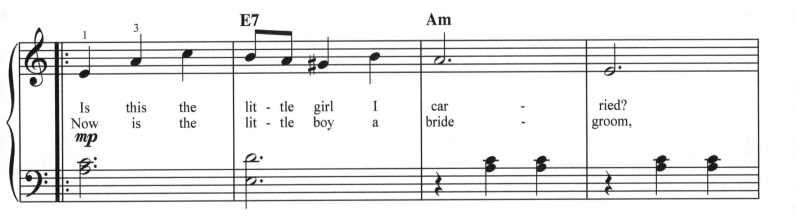

Is this the lit-tle girl I car- ried?
Now is the lit-tle boy a bride- groom,

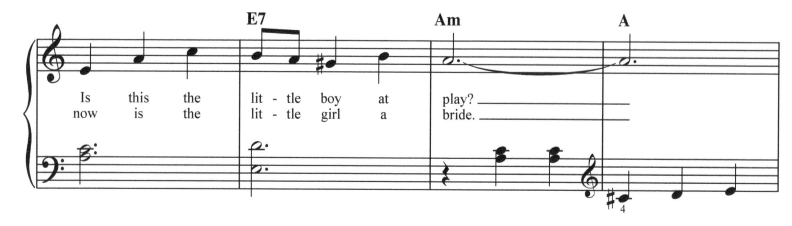

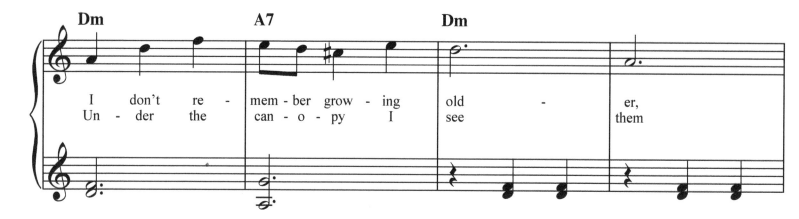

When did he grow to be so tall? _____
share the sweet wine and break the glass; _____

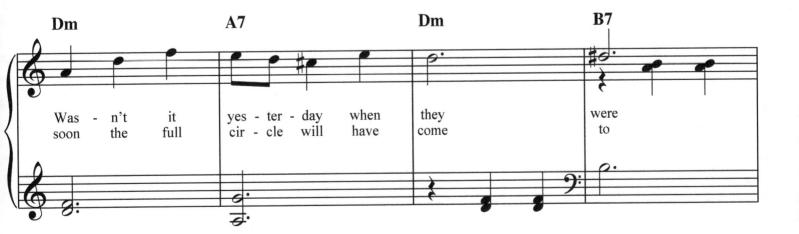

Was - n't it yes - ter - day when they were
soon the full cir - cle will have come to

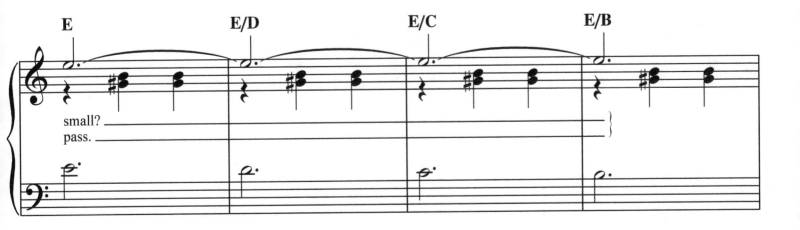

small? _____
pass. _____

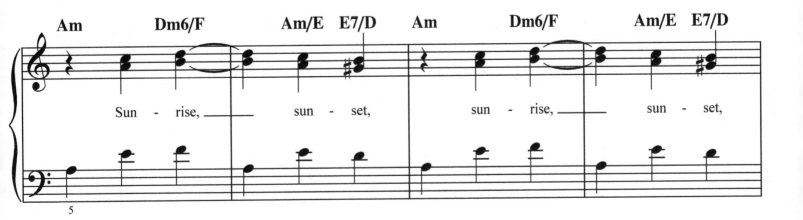

Sun - rise, _____ sun - set, sun - rise, _____ sun - set,

5

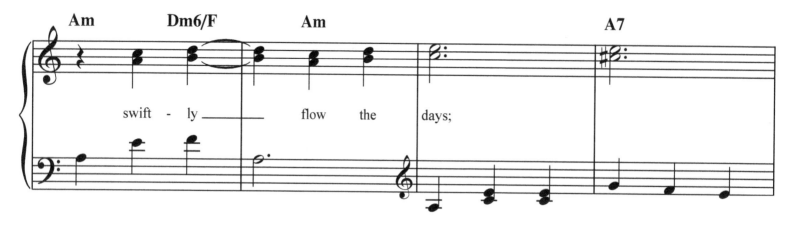

swift - ly _____ flow the days;

seed - lings turn o - ver - night to sun - flow'rs,

blos - som - ing e - ven as we gaze. _____

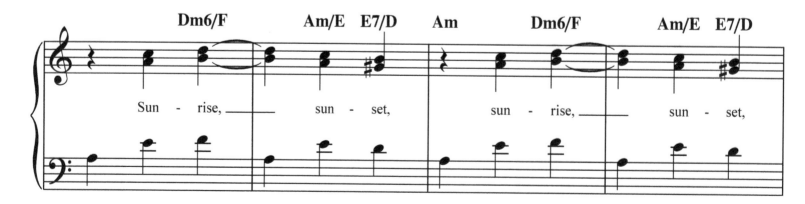

Sun - rise, _____ sun - set, sun - rise, _____ sun - set,

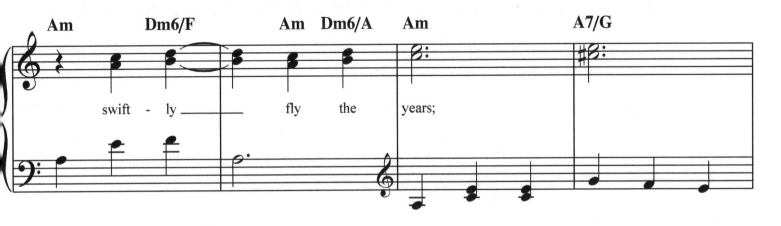

swift - ly _____ fly the years;

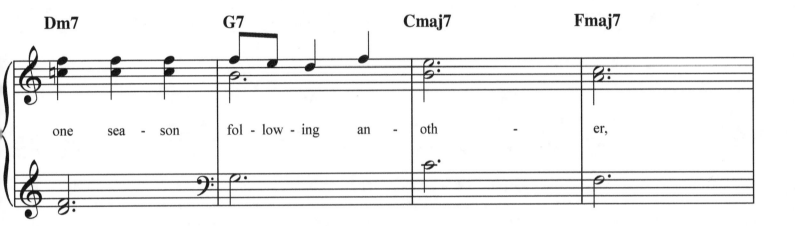

one sea - son fol - low - ing an - oth - er,

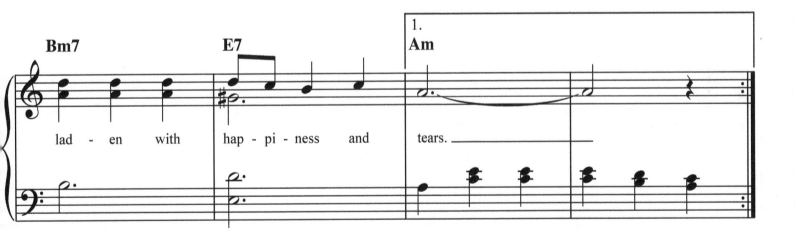

lad - en with hap - pi - ness and tears. _____

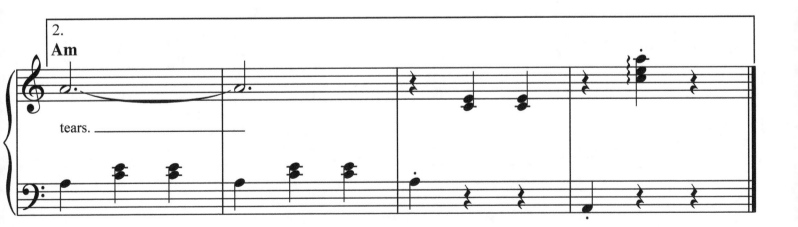

tears. _____

# THANK HEAVEN FOR LITTLE GIRLS

## from GIGI

Words by ALAN JAY LERNER
Music by FREDERICK LOEWE

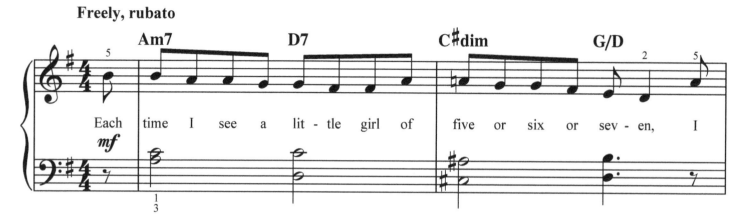

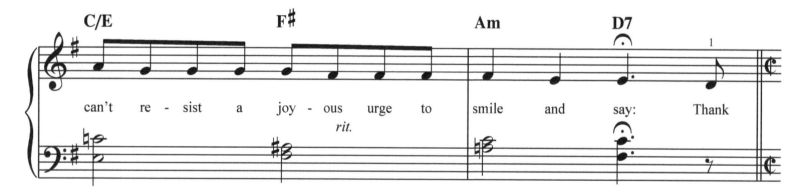

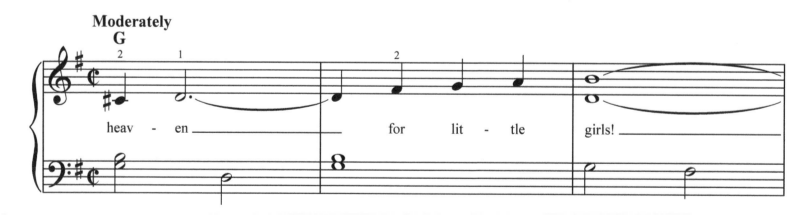

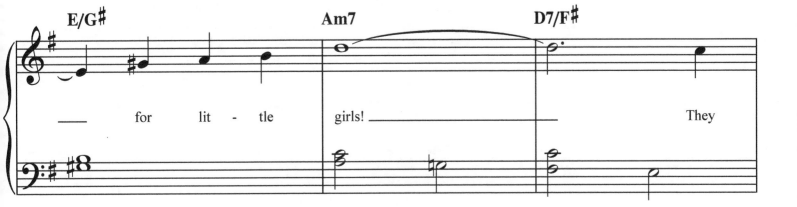

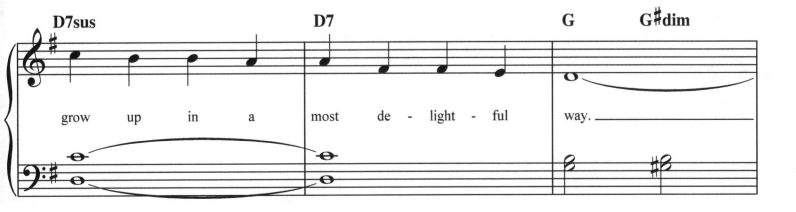

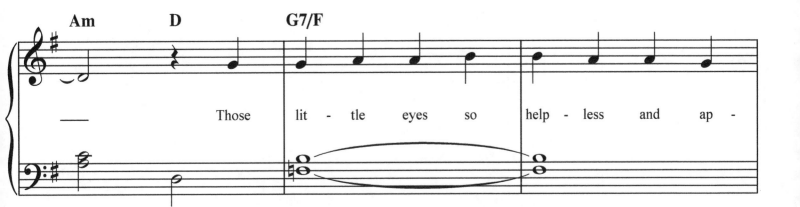

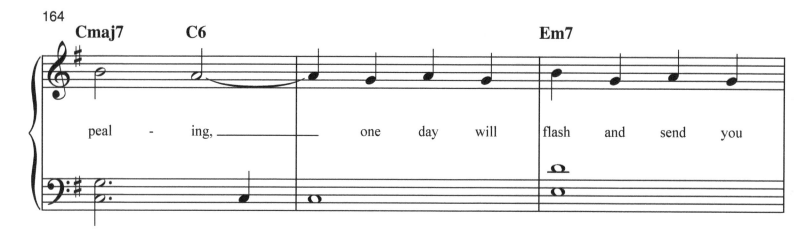

peal - ing, _____ one day will flash and send you

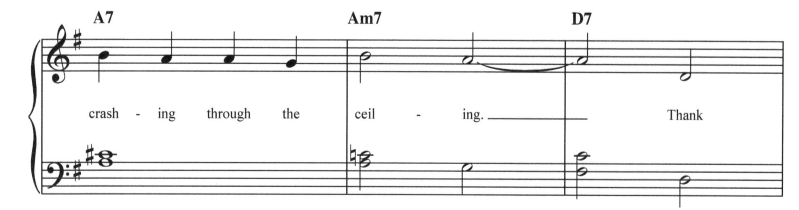

crash - ing through the ceil - ing. _____ Thank

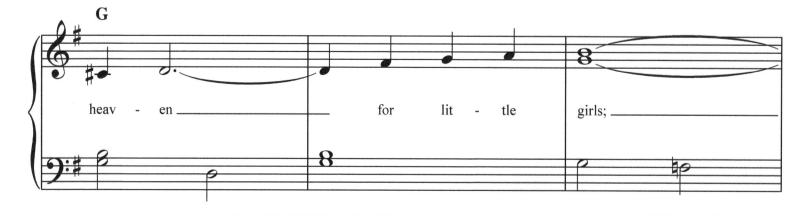

heav - en _____ for lit - tle girls; _____

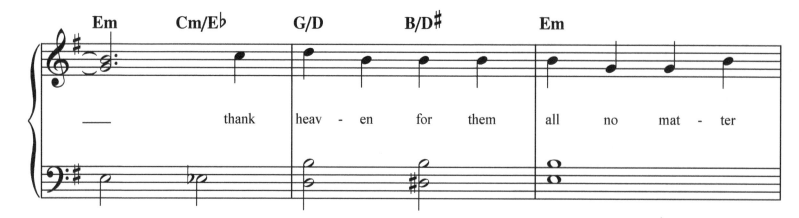

_____ thank heav - en for them all no mat - ter

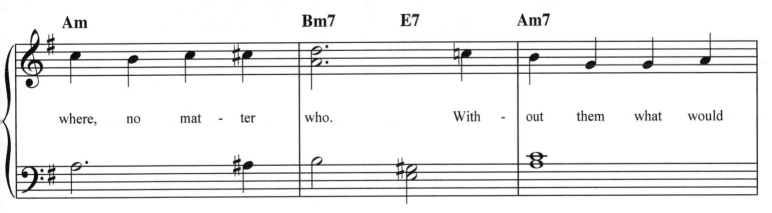

where, no mat - ter who. With - out them what would

lit - tle boys do? _____ Thank heav - en, _____

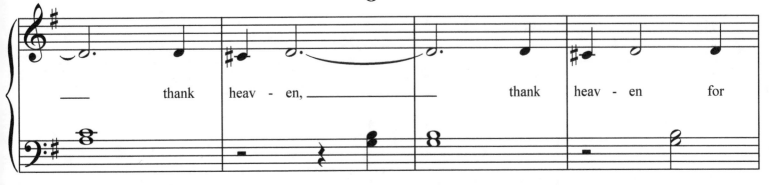

___ thank heav - en, _____ thank heav - en for

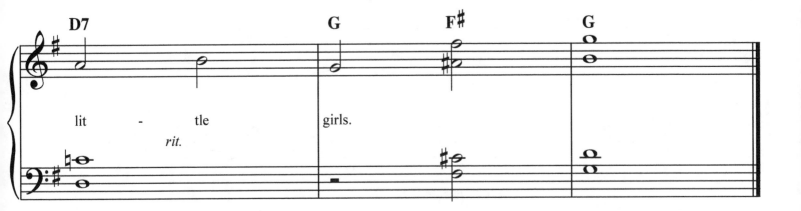

lit - tle girls.

*rit.*

# THIS NEARLY WAS MINE

**from SOUTH PACIFIC**

Lyrics by OSCAR HAMMERSTEIN II
Music by RICHARD RODGERS

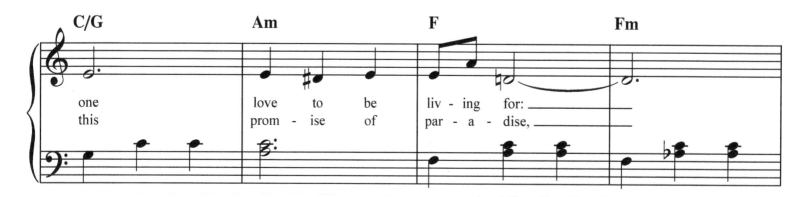

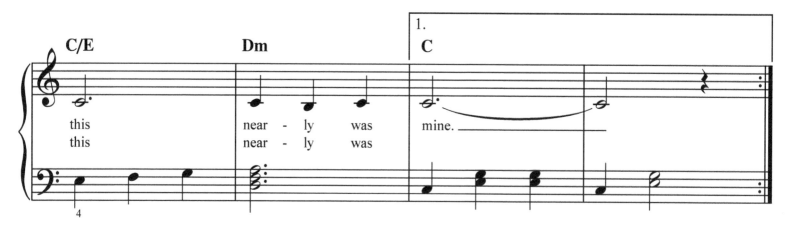

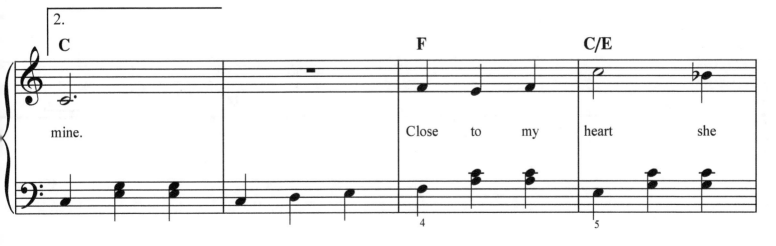

mine. Close to my heart she

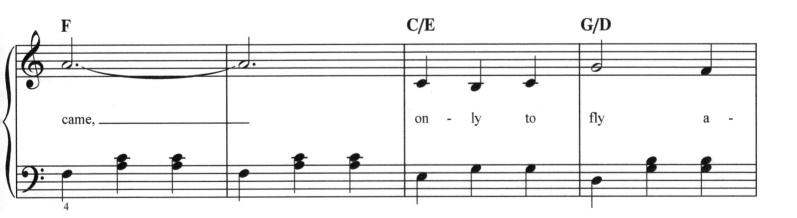

came, on - ly to fly a -

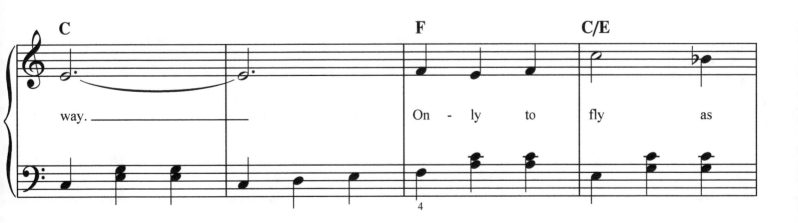

way. On - ly to fly as

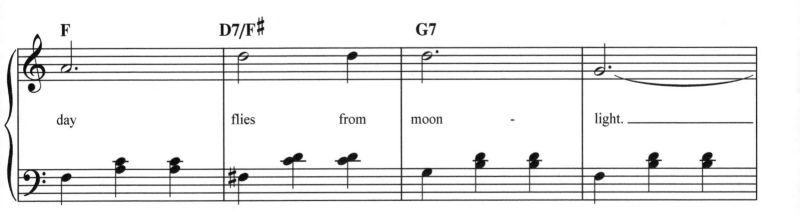

day flies from moon - light.

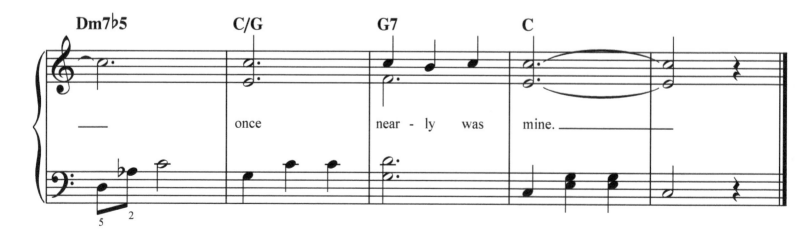

# TOMORROW
## from the Musical Production ANNIE

Lyric by MARTIN CHARNIN
Music by CHARLES STROUSE

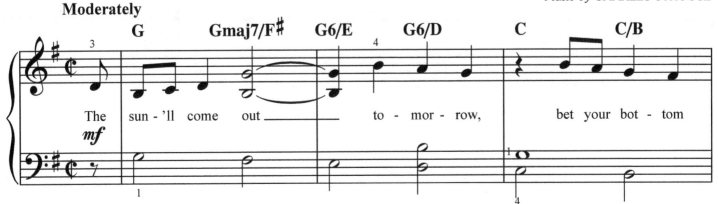

The sun-'ll come out _____ to - mor - row, bet your bot - tom

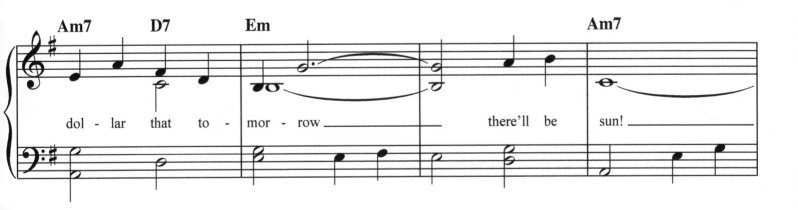

dol - lar that to - mor - row _____ there'll be sun! _____

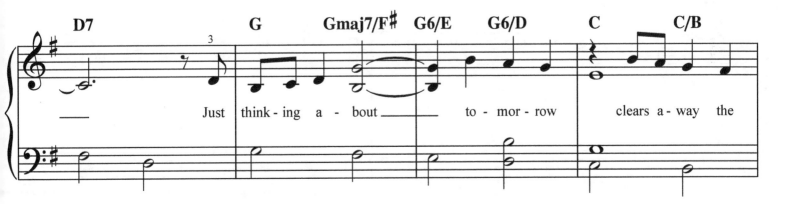

_____ Just think - ing a - bout _____ to - mor - row clears a - way the

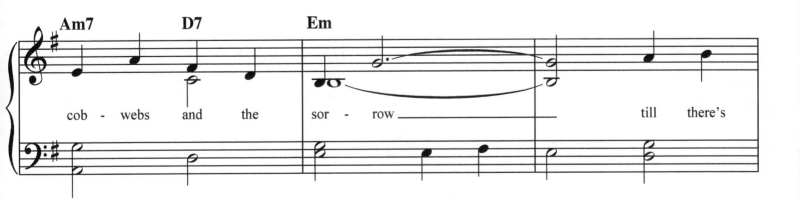

cob - webs and the sor - row _____ till there's

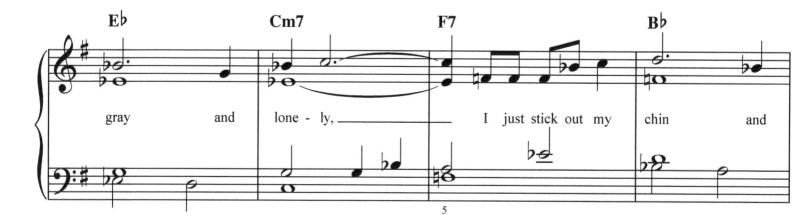

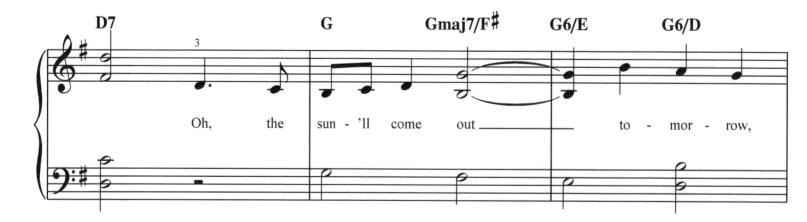

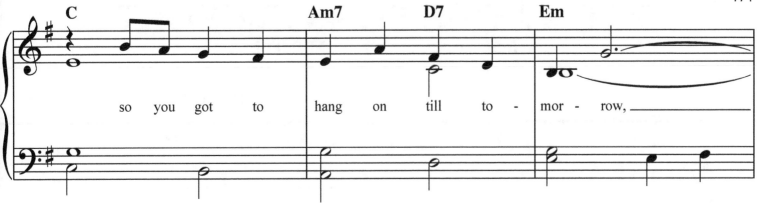

so you got to hang on till to - mor - row, _____

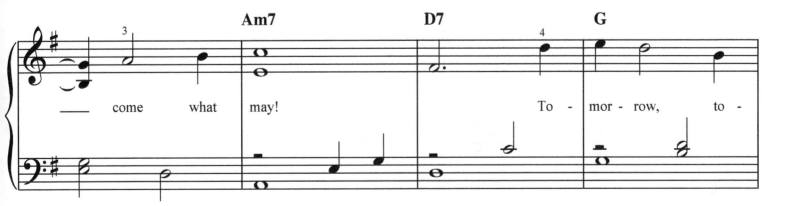

_____ come what may! To - mor - row, to -

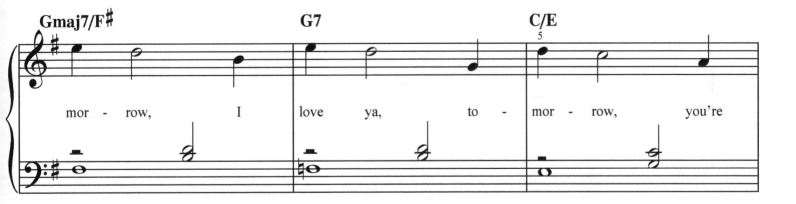

mor - row, I love ya, to - mor - row, you're

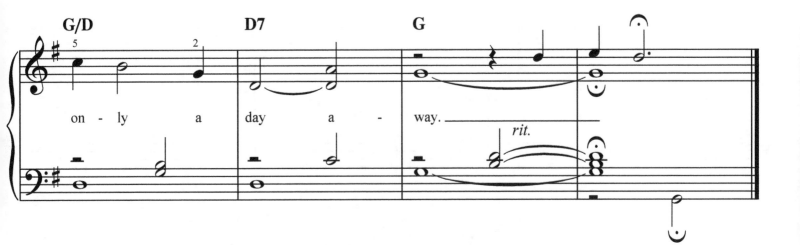

on - ly a day a - way. _____ *rit.*

# TOO CLOSE FOR COMFORT

## from the Musical MR. WONDERFUL

Words and Music by JERRY BOCK,
LARRY HOLOFCENER and GEORGE WEISS

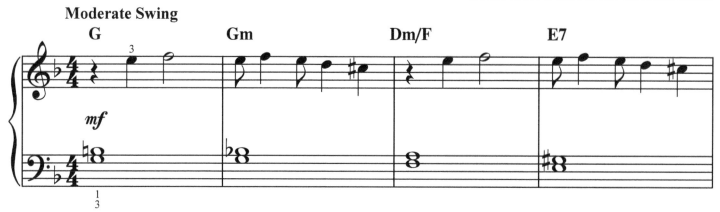

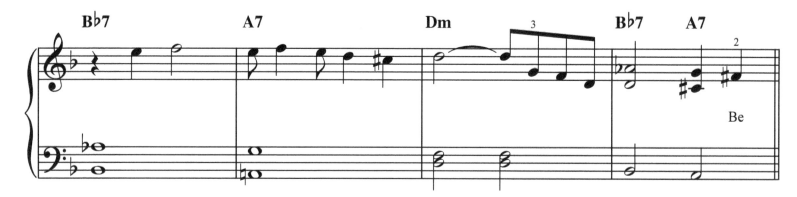

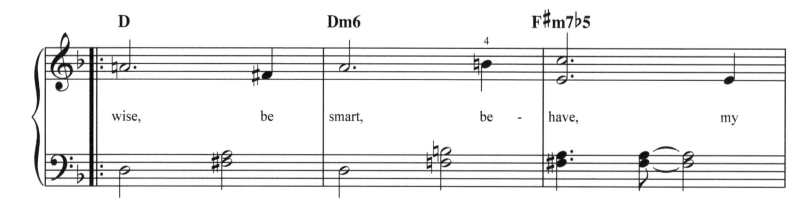

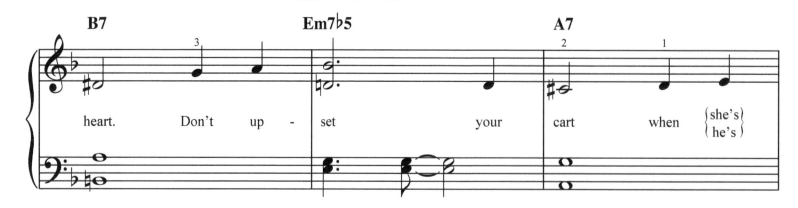

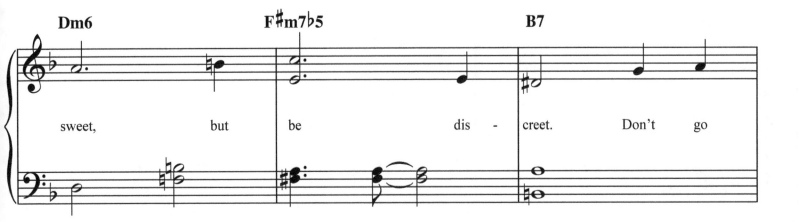

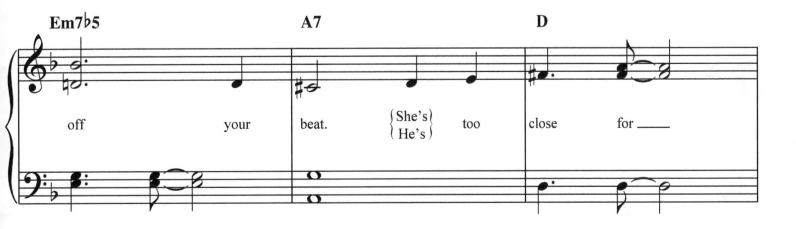

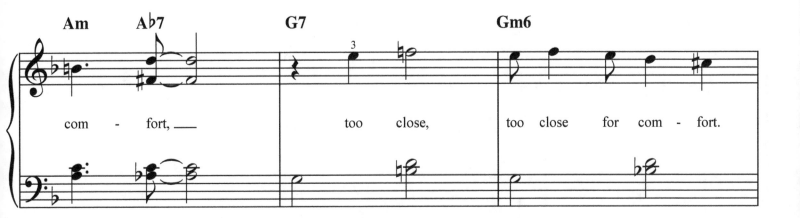

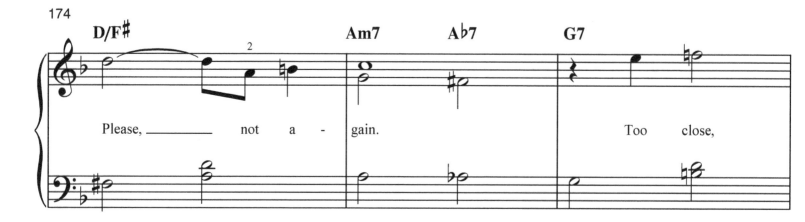

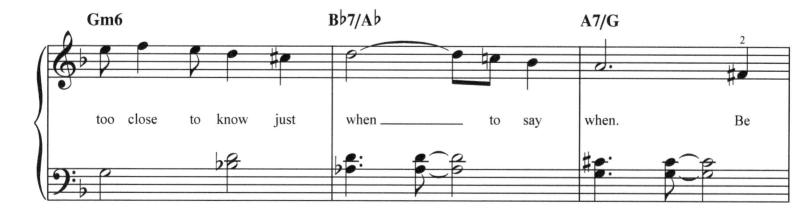

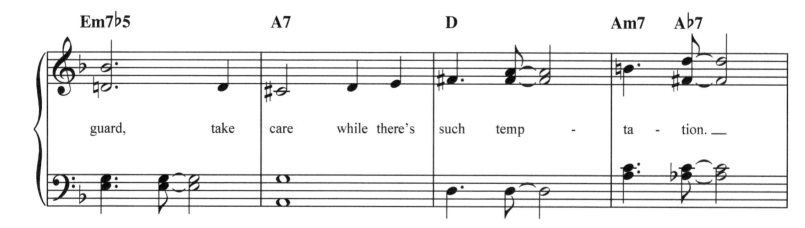

One thing | leads to an - oth - er, | too late

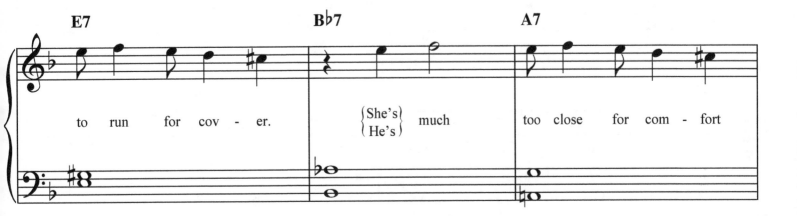

to run for cov - er. | {She's} {He's} much | too close for com - fort

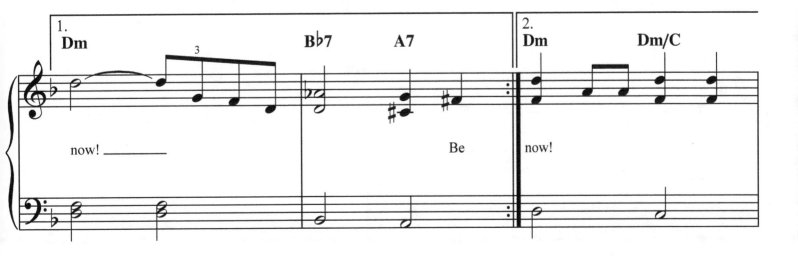

now! _____ | Be | now!

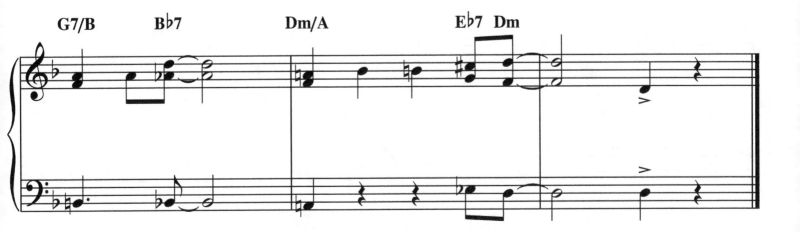

# TRY TO REMEMBER

**from THE FANTASTICKS**

Words by TOM JONES
Music by HARVEY SCHMIDT

**Slowly, with tenderness**

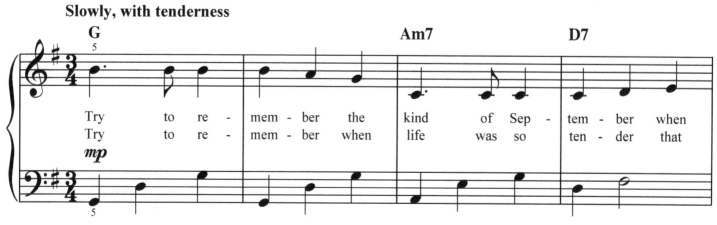

Try to re-mem-ber the kind of Sep-tem-ber when
Try to re-mem-ber when life was so ten-der that

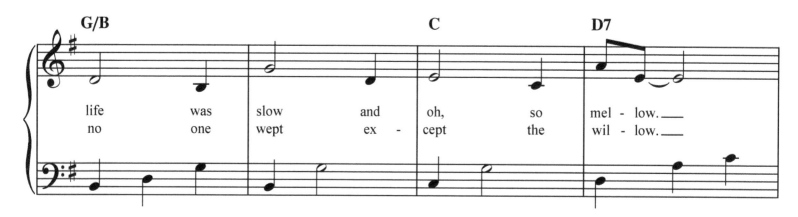

life was slow and oh, so mel-low.___
no one wept ex-cept the wil-low.___

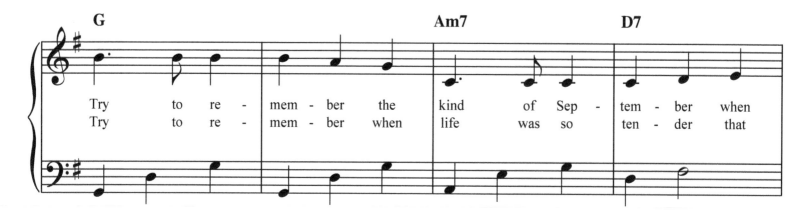

Try to re-mem-ber the kind of Sep-tem-ber when
Try to re-mem-ber when life was so ten-der that

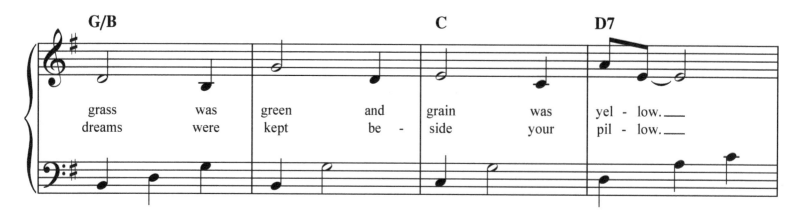

grass was green and grain was yel-low.___
dreams were kept be-side your pil-low.___

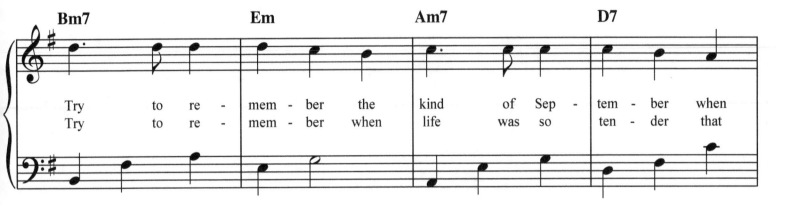

**Bm7**      **Em**      **Am7**      **D7**

Try to re - mem - ber the kind of Sep - tem - ber when
Try to re - mem - ber when life was so ten - der that

**Gmaj7**      **Cmaj7**      **F**      **D7**

you were a ten - der and cal - low fel - low.___
love was an em - ber a - bout to bil - low.___

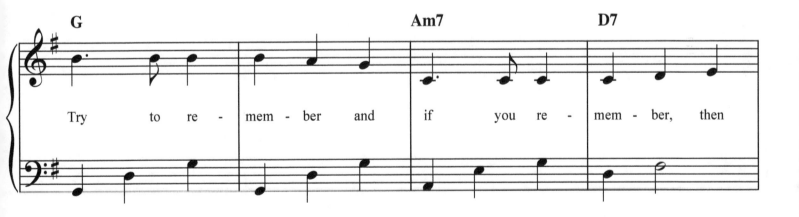

**G**      **Am7**      **D7**

Try to re - mem - ber and if you re - mem - ber, then

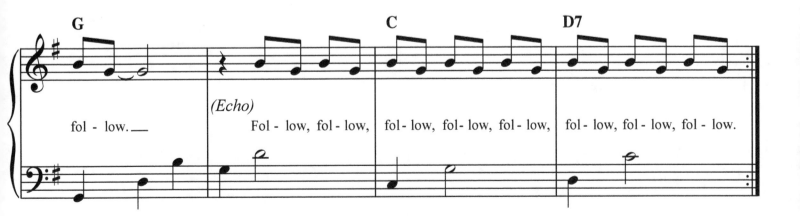

**G**      **C**      **D7**

fol - low.___      *(Echo)* Fol - low, fol - low, fol - low, fol - low, fol - low, fol - low, fol - low, fol - low.

Deep in De - cem - ber, it's nice to re - mem - ber, al -

though you know the snow will fol - low. __

Deep in De - cem - ber, it's nice to re - mem - ber with -

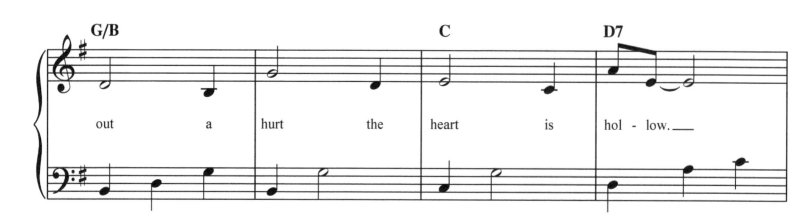

out a hurt the heart is hol - low. __

179

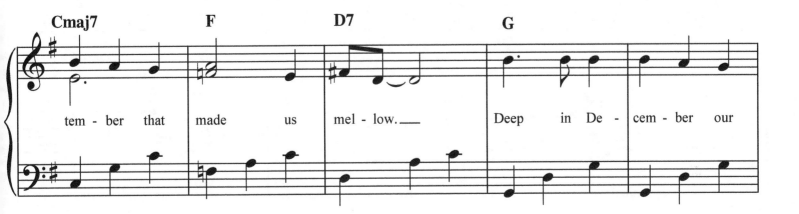

# WHAT I DID FOR LOVE

**from A CHORUS LINE**

Music by MARVIN HAMLISCH
Lyric by EDWARD KLEBAN

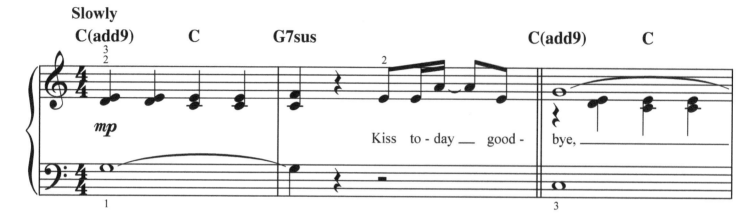

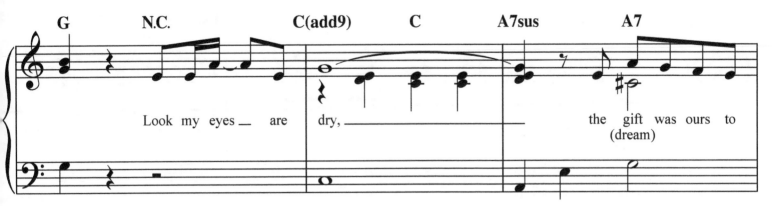

Look my eyes ___ are dry, _____ the gift was ours to (dream)

bor - row. _____ It's as if ___ we al - ways

knew, but I won't for - get what I did for love,

___ what I did for love.

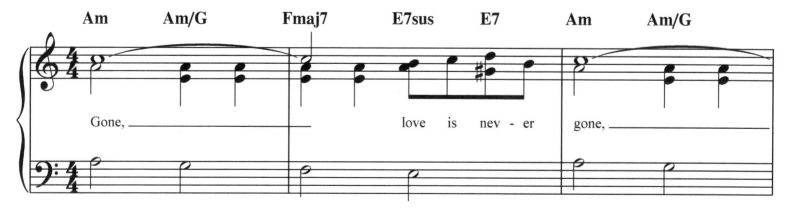

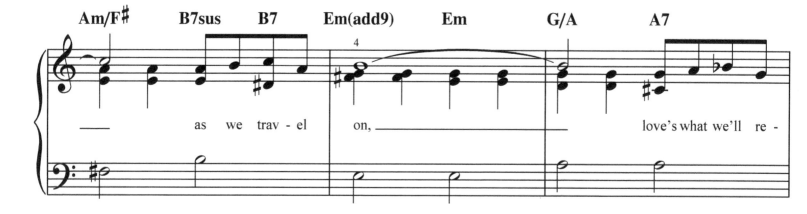

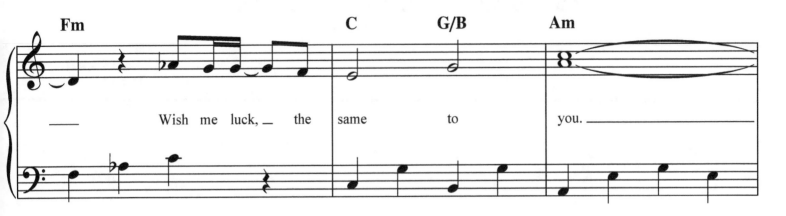

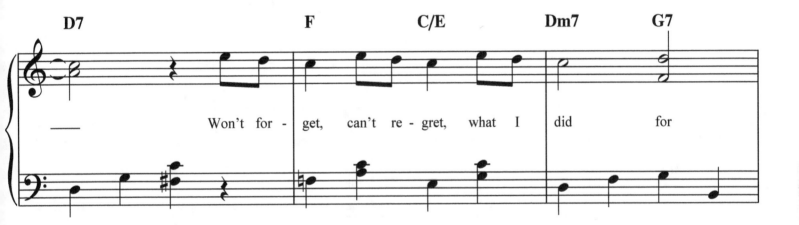

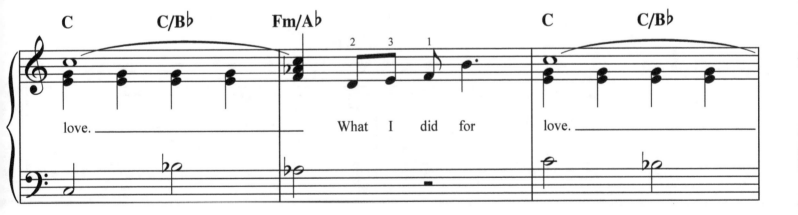

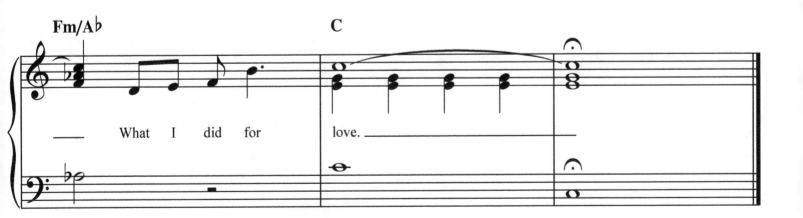

# A WONDERFUL GUY

## from SOUTH PACIFIC

Lyrics by OSCAR HAMMERSTEIN II
Music by RICHRD RODGERS

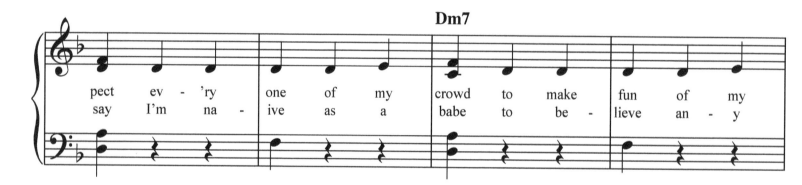

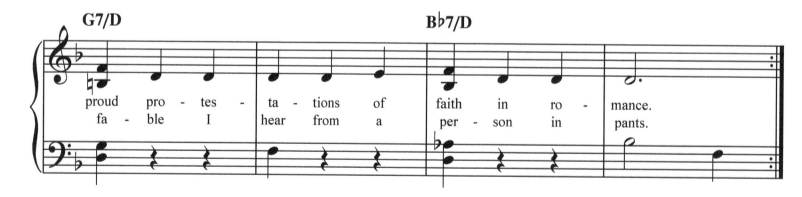

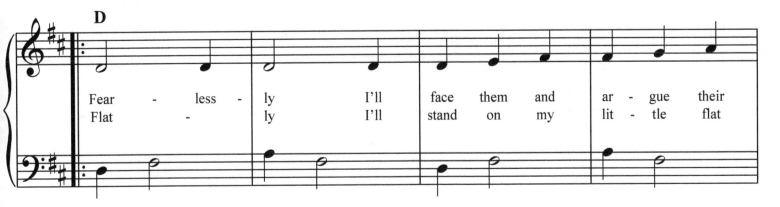

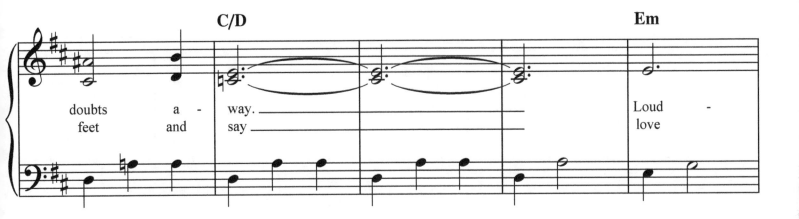

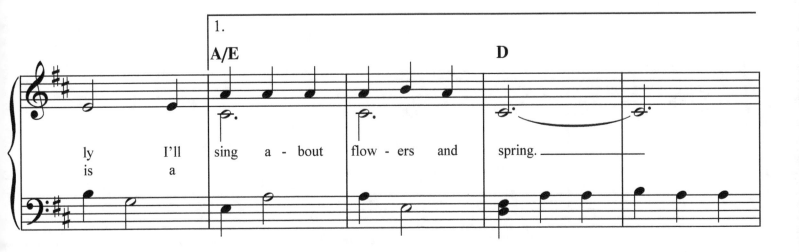

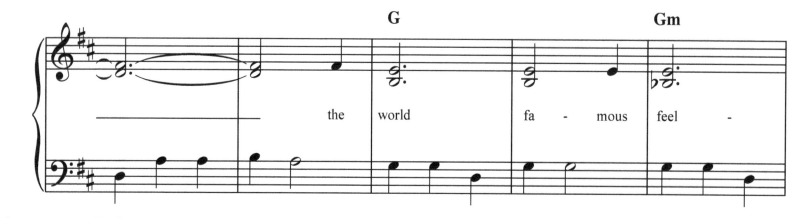

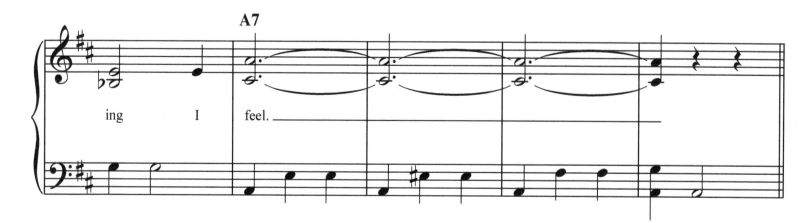

187

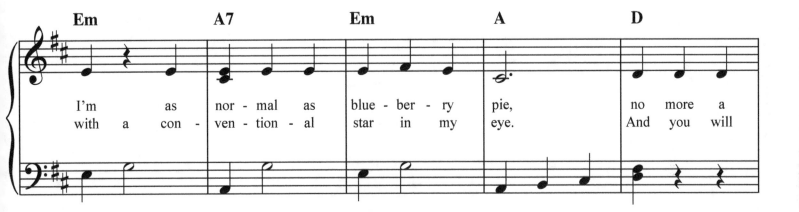

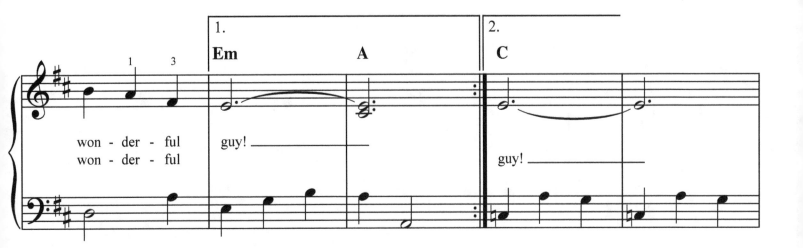

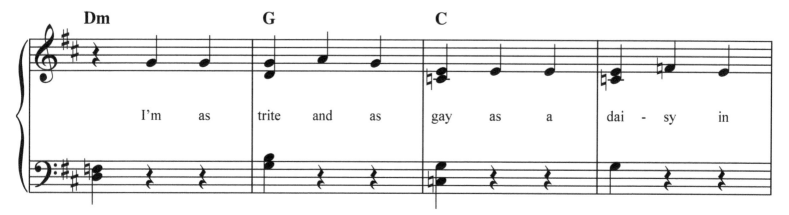

I'm as trite and as gay as a dai - sy in

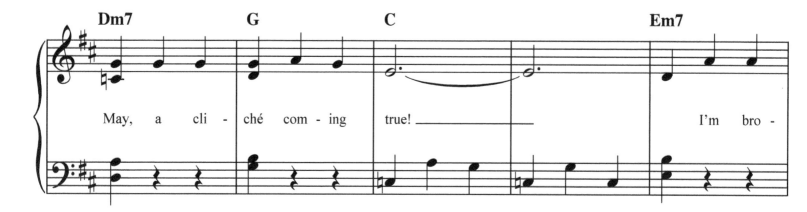

May, a cli - ché com - ing true! ___ I'm bro -

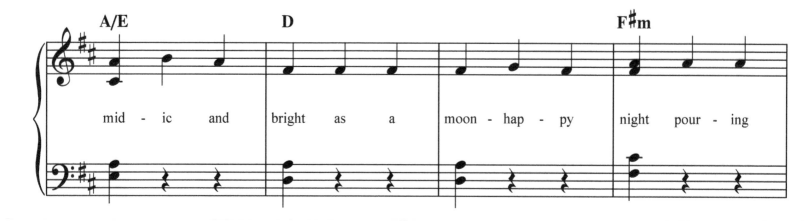

mid - ic and bright as a moon-hap - py night pour - ing

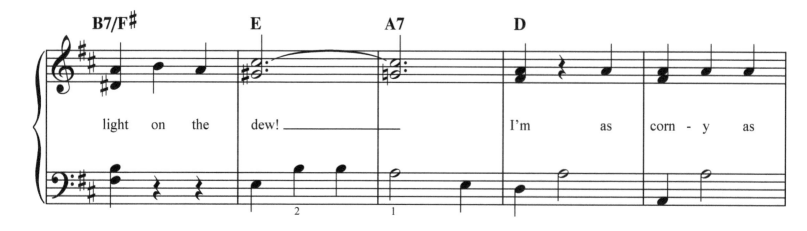

light on the dew! ___ I'm as corn - y as

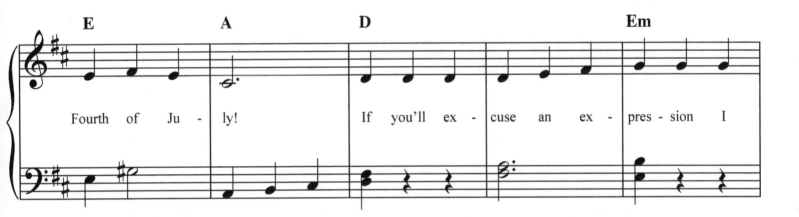

Kan - sas in Au - gust, high as a flag on the

**E**        **A**        **D**                          **Em**

Fourth of Ju - ly! If you'll ex - cuse an ex - pres - sion I

**A**        **D**        **Em**        **D/F♯**        **D+/F♯**

use, I'm in love, I'm in love, I'm in love, I'm in love, I'm in

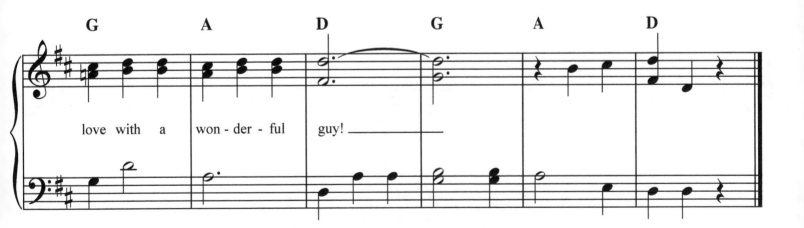

**G**        **A**        **D**        **G**        **A**        **D**

love with a won - der - ful guy! _____

# WHAT KIND OF FOOL AM I?

## from the Musical Production STOP THE WORLD – I WANT TO GET OFF

Words and Music by LESLIE BRICUSSE
and ANTHONY NEWLEY

**Moderately slow**

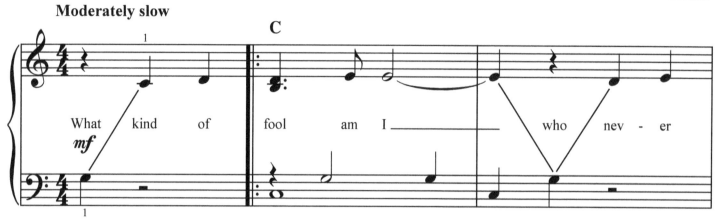

What kind of fool am I ___ who nev - er

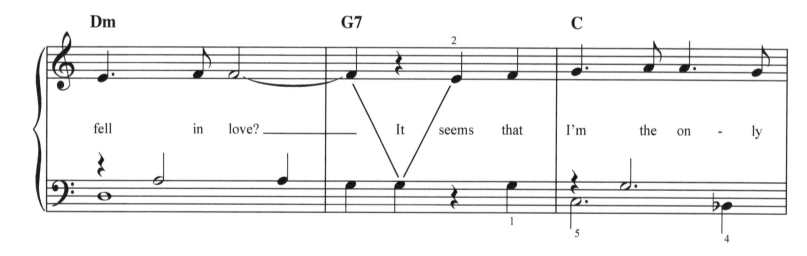

fell in love? ___ It seems that I'm the on - ly

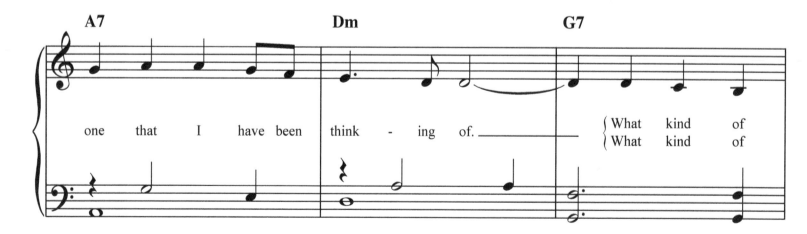

one that I have been think - ing of. ___ { What kind of
{ What kind of

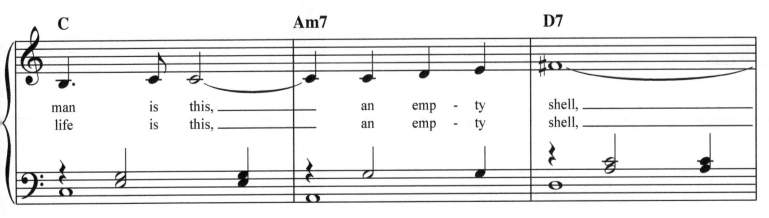

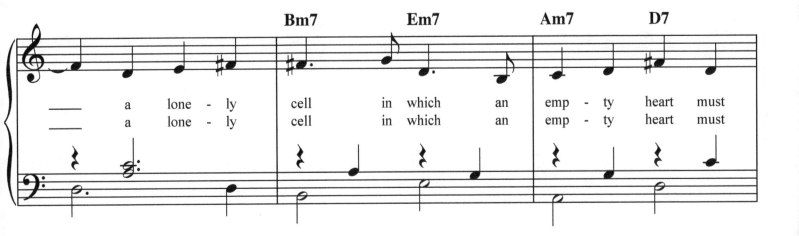

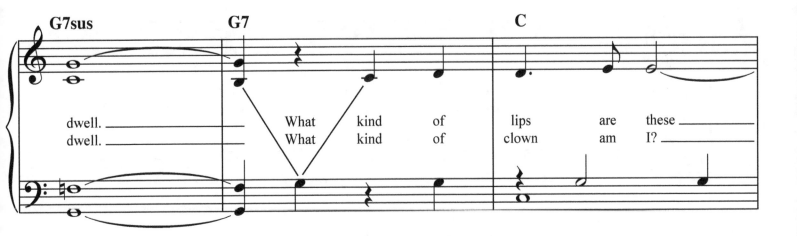

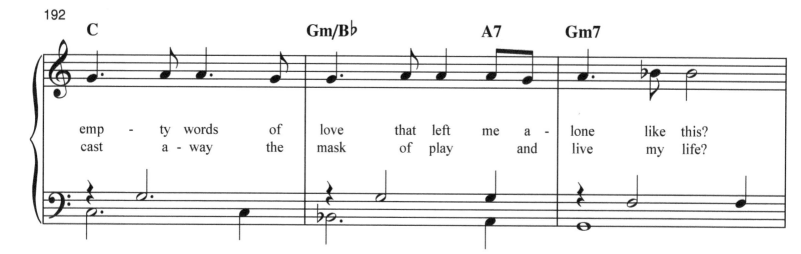

emp - ty words of love that left me a - lone like this?
cast a - way of the mask of play me and live my life?

Why can't I fall in love like an - y
Why can't I fall in love 'til I don't

oth - er man, and may - be then I'll know what kind of fool I
give a damn, and may - be then I'll know what kind of fool I

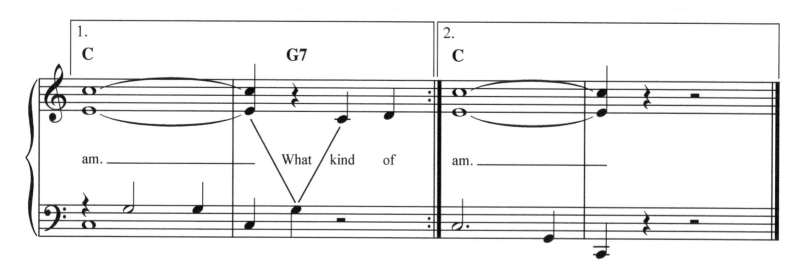

1.
am. _____ What kind of

2.
am. _____